George Swinnock

St. Mary's tower, built in 1630,
in Rickmansworth, Hertfordshire

(Developed from the survey drawing of 1985 by Graham D. Martin)

"Trading and Thriving in Godliness":
The Piety of George Swinnock

Introduced and Edited by
J. Stephen Yuille

Reformation Heritage Books
Grand Rapids, Michigan

Trading and Thriving in Godliness

© 2008 by J. Stephen Yuille

Published by
Reformation Heritage Books
2965 Leonard St., NE
Grand Rapids, MI 49525
616-977-0599 / Fax: 616-285-3246
e-mail: orders@heritagebooks.org
website: www.heritagebooks.org

Library of Congress Cataloging-in-Publication Data

Swinnock, George, 1627-1673.
  Trading and thriving in godliness : the piety of George Swinnock /
edited and introduced by J. Stephen Yuille ; with a foreword by
Anthony N.S. La.
    p. cm. -- (Profiles in reformed spirituality)
  ISBN 978-1-60178-041-6 (pbk. : alk. paper)
  1. Puritans--Sermons. 2. Sermons, English--17th century. I. Yuille,
J. Stephen, 1968- II. Title.
  BX9315.S95 2008
  252'.059--dc22
                                        2008013954

---

*For additional Reformed literature, both new and used, request a free book
list from Reformation Heritage Books at the above address.*

For Michael Haykin
– Professor, Colleague, Friend

PROFILES IN REFORMED SPIRITUALITY
series editors—Joel R. Beeke and Michael A.G. Haykin

Other Books in the Series:

Table of Contents

Section Four: The Pursuit of Godliness

Section Five: The Nature of Godliness

Section Six: The Means to Godliness

Section Seven: The Motives to Godliness

Profiles in Reformed Spirituality

Charles Dickens' famous line in *A Tale of Two Cities*—
"it was the best of times, it was the worst of times"
—seems well suited to western Evangelicalism since
the 1960s. On the one hand, these decades have seen
much for which to praise God and to rejoice. In His
goodness and grace, for instance, Reformed truth is
no longer a house under siege. Growing numbers
identify themselves theologically with what we hold
to be biblical truth, namely, Reformed theology and
piety. And yet, as an increasing number of Reformed
authors have noted, there are many sectors of the
surrounding western Evangelicalism that are characterized by great shallowness and a trivialization of the
weighty things of God. So much of Evangelical worship seems barren. And when it comes to spirituality,
there is little evidence of the riches of our heritage as
Reformed Evangelicals.

As it was at the time of the Reformation, when the
watchword was *ad fontes*—"back to the sources"—so
it is now: the way forward is backward. We need to
go back to the spiritual heritage of Reformed Evangelicalism to find the pathway forward. We cannot
live in the past; to attempt to do so would be anti-
quarianism. But our Reformed forebearers in the faith

can teach us much about Christianity, its doctrines, its passions, and its fruit.

And they can serve as our role models. As R. C. Sproul has noted of such giants as Augustine, Martin Luther, John Calvin, and Jonathan Edwards: "These men all were conquered, overwhelmed, and spiritually intoxicated by their vision of the holiness of God. Their minds and imaginations were captured by the majesty of God the Father. Each of them possessed a profound affection for the sweetness and excellence of Christ. There was in each of them a singular and unswerving loyalty to Christ that spoke of a citizenship in heaven that was always more precious to them than the applause of men."[1]

To be sure, we would not dream of placing these men and their writings alongside the Word of God. John Jewel (1522–1571), the Anglican apologist, once stated: "What say we of the fathers, Augustine, Ambrose, Jerome, Cyprian?... They were learned men, and learned fathers; the instruments of the mercy of God, and vessels full of grace. We despise them not, we read them, we reverence them, and give thanks unto God for them. Yet...we may not make them the foundation and warrant of our conscience: we may not put our trust in them. Our trust is in the name of the Lord."[2]

Seeking then both to honor the past and yet not idolize it, we are issuing these books in the series

---

1. "An Invaluable Heritage," *Tabletalk*, 23, no. 10 (October 1999): 5–6.

2. Cited in Barrington R. White, "Why Bother with History?" *Baptist History and Heritage*, 4, no. 2 (July 1969): 85.

Profiles in Reformed Spirituality. The design is to introduce the spirituality and piety of the Reformed tradition by presenting descriptions of the lives of notable Christians with select passages from their works. This combination of biographical sketches and collected portions from primary sources gives a taste of the subjects' contributions to our spiritual heritage and some direction as to how the reader can find further edification through their works. It is the hope of the publishers that this series will provide riches for those areas where we are poor and light of day where we are stumbling in the deepening twilight.

—Joel R. Beeke
Michael A. G. Haykin

Foreword

George Swinnock is not exactly well known. Even many who have an interest in the Puritans will not have heard of him. A Banner of Truth reprint in 1992 made the five volumes of his works available, but in comparison with giants like Perkins, Owen, and Baxter, he is relatively unknown. I have to confess that until Stephen Yuille approached me as a potential supervisor at the beginning of the millennium (the third millennium that is, not the millennium of Revelation 20) I had not myself heard of him. I am grateful to Stephen Yuille for having introduced me to this Puritan and reading the drafts of his Ph.D. proved to be spiritually, as well as academically, stimulating. Swinnock has no distinctive perspectives to offer and one feature of the Ph.D. thesis was to demonstrate that Swinnock was an exponent of the mainstream Puritan consensus. This is no problem. We do not always need to be learning something new. Simply to be reminded of the old truths, forcefully and eloquently stated, can be very helpful.

Few will buy the five volumes of Swinnock's works. Even fewer will read them. The rest of us can be very grateful to Stephen Yuille for enabling us to sample some of his gems in a single volume. This certainly deserves a wide readership. In addition, maybe some will be so entranced that they will go on to join the select company of those who have engaged with the five-volume set.

If anyone is qualified to make the selection of passages from George Swinnock, it is Stephen Yuille. During the five years of his thesis studies, he immersed himself in Swinnock's writings. The thesis was very well received by the examiners and has since been published—an honor that is by no means granted to all theses.

Therefore, I am very happy to commend this volume and pray that it will be for the edification of many.

—Anthony N. S. Lane

Acknowledgements

— ◦«(•)»◦ —

I want to thank my wife, Alison, and my daughter, Laura, for their unwavering encouragement. Next to the Lord Jesus, they are my greatest joy!

I also want to express my sincere thanks to Dr. Michael Haykin and Dr. Joel Beeke for their invitation to contribute to this series: *Profiles in Reformed Spirituality*. I have enjoyed the volumes to date, and I count it a great privilege to add George Swinnock to their number.

Up until July 2007 (when I turned my attention to completing the present work), I had not given Swinnock a glance since completing my Ph.D. thesis on his theology and spirituality in April 2006. After a fifteen-month hiatus, it was refreshing to read him anew. It was like a chance meeting with an old friend—we picked up right where we had left off! The words of James Hamilton beautifully sum up my admiration for Swinnock: "Except to a few collectors, the writings of Swinnock are almost unknown; but we confess that we have rejoiced in them as those that find great spoil. So pithy and pungent, and so practical, few books are more fitted to keep the attention awake, and few so richly reward it."[1]

1. George Swinnock, *Door of Salvation Opened by the Key of Regen-*

Indeed, I have found "great spoil" in Swinnock's writings. In *The Incomparableness of God*, he enlarged my vision of God's glory and majesty. In *The Door of Salvation Opened by the Key of Regeneration*, he increased my understanding of what it means to be born again. In *Heaven and Hell Epitomized* and *The Fading of the Flesh*, he challenged my concept of Christian discipleship. However, it is *The Christian Man's Calling*, to which I am most indebted. It is an enormous treatise, accounting for close to half of Swinnock's literary output. In the words of James Nichol, "[It] is one of the fullest, and, we venture to think, one of the best exhibitions of the gospel in its application to the ordinary affairs of life. There are few better works of practical religion in our language."[2] Through this treatise, Swinnock heightened my appreciation of what it means to godly. For this, I am thankful.

J. Stephen Yuille
Peterborough, Ontario
January 2008

---

eration; or *A Treatise Containing the Nature, Necessity, Marks and Means of Regeneration: as also the Duty of the Regenerate,* in *The Works of George Swinnock,* ed. J. Nichol. (London, 1868; rpt., Edinburgh: Banner of Truth, 1992), 5:xii. Except for his biography of Thomas Wilson, all references to Swinnock's treatises are taken from this set of his works.

2. Swinnock, *Door of Salvation,* 5:xiv. James Nichol was the publisher of Swinnock's collected works (1868).

He that is ever trading and thriving in godliness, need not fear that he shall prove a bankrupt.
                                    —George Swinnock,
                              Christian Man's Calling, 1:25

Herein, reader, I have drawn the saint's picture, by which thou mayest perceive somewhat of the beauty of his person, and the excellency and loveliness of his life. This indeed is the true life, all other but the shadow of living.
                                    —George Swinnock,
                            Christian Man's Calling, 1:389

St. Mary's tower in Rickmansworth

(Photograph: Allan Swann)

The Piety of George Swinnock
(1627–1673)

According to Edmund Calamy,[1] George Swinnock
was a "serious, warm…practical, useful preacher."[2]
He was born in 1627 at Maidstone, Kent. He gradu-
ated with a B.A. from Cambridge University and an
M.A. from Oxford University. Upon receiving the
latter, he resigned his fellowship to become vicar at
St. Mary's chapel, Rickmansworth, Hertfordshire.
After eleven years, he moved to St. Nicholas' chapel,
Great Kimble, Buckinghamshire. Upon his ejection
for nonconformity in 1662, he entered the household
of Richard Hampden to minister as family chaplain.[3]
With the easing of political restrictions in 1672, he
returned to his home of Maidstone to become pastor.
He occupied this position for less than a year, dying
at the age of forty-six.[4]

---

1. Edmund Calamy (1671–1732) produced a history of the min-
isters ejected from the Church of England by the Act of Uniformity
in 1662.

2. Edmund Calamy, *The Nonconformist's Memorial* (London:
Printed for W. Harris, 1775), 1:303–304.

3. Richard Hampden was the father of John Hampden—famous
for his support of the parliamentary forces during the English Civil
War.

4. See *Oxford Dictionary of National Biography*, eds. H.C.G. Matthew
and Brian Harrison (Oxford: Oxford University Press, 2004), s.v.

Apart from these few details, we know very little of Swinnock. There is no available funeral sermon or collection of letters, and there are scant references in the writings of his contemporaries. There is, however, plenty we can learn about Swinnock's piety from his collected sermons and treatises.

The Context of Swinnock's Piety

Swinnock was Puritan in his piety. Three key influences contributed to this.

Robert Swinnock

We know that Swinnock spent much of his childhood in the home of his uncle. When speaking of his cousin, Caleb Swinnock, he comments, "I had the happiness some time to be brought up with him in his father's, Mr. Robert Swinnock's, family."[5] Whatever the circumstances surrounding this stay, Swinnock describes it in a positive light as he recalls that his uncle's house "had holiness to the Lord written upon it." He explains:

> His manner was to pray twice a day by himself, once or twice a day with his wife, and twice a day with his family, besides singing psalms, reading, and expounding Scriptures, which morning and evening were minded. The Sabbath he dedicated wholly to God's service, and did not only himself, but took care that all within his gate should spend the day in secret and private duties, and in atten-

---

5. George Swinnock, *Christian Man's Calling; or A Treatise of Making Religion Ones Business,* in *The Works of George Swinnock,* 3:409.

dance on public ordinances; of their proficiency by the last, he would take an account upon their return from the assembly.[6]

It was in this "school of religion"[7] that Swinnock lived until he departed for Cambridge University in 1643, when he was sixteen. Given the fact that the first sixteen years of life are crucial in the formation of a person's character and convictions, it is certain that his uncle's piety greatly influenced Swinnock.

Thomas Wilson
This influence intensified with the arrival of Thomas Wilson (1601–1653) at Otham, Kent.[8] The events surrounding his appointment as pastor are noteworthy. Swinnock mentions that "many serious understanding Christians" at Maidstone, near Otham, were "much troubled and dejected at the deadness and dullness of that Ministry under which they lived."[9] Upon the death of the preacher at Otham, the responsibility for finding a replacement fell upon Robert Swinnock, who was an alderman at Maidstone. He was determined to bring a "godly" minister to a church so close to home. Having heard Wilson preach elsewhere, he invited him to Otham. From that time, the "seri-

---

6. Swinnock, *Christian Man's Calling,* 3:409.

7. Swinnock, *Christian Man's Calling,* 3:409.

8. In 1643, Wilson became a member of the Westminster Assembly. Swinnock remarks that Wilson "was much esteemed in the Assembly, for his solid judicious Discourses as occasion was offered, and his meek humble behaviour." George Swinnock, *The Life and Death of Mr. Thomas Wilson, Minister of Maidstone, in the County of Kent, M.A.* (London, 1672), 22.

9. Swinnock, *Life and Death of Mr. Wilson,* 8.

ous" Christians journeyed from Maidstone to hear Wilson's sermons. Furthermore, it was Wilson's custom to have supper every Sunday at the home of his patron.[10] This means that, from infancy, Swinnock was raised under Wilson's preaching and catechizing. At the time of Wilson's death in 1653, Swinnock remarks to the inhabitants of Maidstone: "I must ingenuously acknowledge, that it was a great mercy to me that I was born amongst you, and brought up under as pious and powerful a ministry there, as most in England."[11]

Emmanuel College
The last noteworthy influence is Emmanuel College, Cambridge University, for which Swinnock departed at age sixteen. This college was originally founded "for the education of young men in all piety and good letters and especially Holy Writ and Theology, that being thus instructed they may hereafter teach true and pure religion, refute all errors and heresies, and by the shining example of a blameless life excite all men to virtue."[12] From the outset, it was known for its Puritan sympathies.[13] J. C. Ryle explains:

Sir Walter Mildmay of Chelmsford, in Essex, was

---

10. Swinnock, *Life and Death of Mr. Wilson*, 29.

11. Swinnock, *Christian Man's Calling*, 3:408.

12. "Emmanuel Statutes" as quoted in C. Brooke and R. Highfield, eds., *Oxford and Cambridge* (Cambridge University Press, 1988), 162.

13. It was also known for the number of leading Puritan divines who passed through its doors; e.g., Joseph Hall, Edward Reynolds, Stephen Marshall, Jeremiah Burroughs, Thomas Shepard, Thomas Hooker, John Preston, Stephen Charnock, Ralph Venning, and Thomas Watson.

The front court of Emmanuel College, showing
the chapel with the dining hall to the left.

the founder of Emmanuel College, and even from its very foundation in 1585, it seems to have been notorious for its attachment to Puritan principles. Fuller, in his history of Cambridge, relates that on "Sir Walter Mildmay coming to court, soon after he had founded his college, Queen Elizabeth said to him, 'Sir Walter, I hear you have erected a puritan foundation.' 'No, madam,' saith he, 'far be it from me to countenance anything contrary to your established laws; but I have set an acorn, which, when it becomes an oak, God alone knows what will be the fruit thereof.'[14]

When Swinnock arrived at the college, the entire atmosphere was decidedly Puritan. There is no doubt that his character and convictions were further influenced by this exposure.

The Foundation of Swinnock's Piety
Swinnock's Puritan piety is encapsulated in his concept of the fear of God. He expresses this in terms of Ecclesiastes 12:13, where the preacher declares, "Let us hear the conclusion of the whole matter: Fear God, and keep his commandments: for this is the whole duty of man."[15]

The Covenant Promise
Swinnock defines regeneration as "a work of God's Spirit, whereby he doth, out of his mere good plea-

---

14. J. C. Ryle, "A Biographical Account of the Author" in William Gurnall, *The Christian in Complete Armour: A Treatise of the Saints' War against the Devil* (London: Blackie & Sons, 1864; rpt., Edinburgh: Banner of Truth, 1995), xix.

15. Swinnock, *Christian Man's Calling*, 1:388, 3:167.

sure, for his own glory and the salvation of his elect, at first renew the whole man after his own image by the ministry of the word."[16] This renewal is the restoration of the proper functioning of the soul's faculties so that they are characterized by knowledge, righteousness, and true holiness.[17] In this paradigm, the faculties are inseparable in that the will is determined by the affections, which, in turn, are determined by the mind. Swinnock remarks, "Right knowledge, though it begin at the head, doth not end there, but falls down upon the heart to affect that, and floweth out in the life to order and regulate that."[18] For Swinnock, this restoration of the faculties is that fear promised by God in the everlasting covenant—"And I will make an everlasting covenant with them, that I will not turn away from them, to do them good; but I will put my fear in their hearts, that they shall not depart from me."[19]

The Fear of God and the Mind

According to Swinnock, this fear of God necessarily begins in the mind with "apprehensions of God's infinite majesty."[20] Swinnock appeals to the example of the Israelites, who knew the consequences of offering "polluted bread" to their governor, yet had no difficulty in presenting such sacrifices to God,

---

16. Swinnock, *Door of Salvation*, 5:20.

17. Ephesians 4:24; Colossians 3:10. See Swinnock, *Christian Man's Calling*, 3:359.

18. George Swinnock, *Treatise of the Incomparableness of God in His Being, Attributes, Works and Word: Opened and Applied*, 4:482.

19. Jeremiah 32:40.

20. Swinnock, *Christian Man's Calling*, 1:95.

thereby demonstrating their lack of fear for the "great King."[21] This disrespect was the consequence of their ignorance. From this, Swinnock concludes that it is impossible to fear God without knowing Him.

The psalmist asks, "For who in the heaven can be compared unto the LORD?"[22] For Swinnock, the answer is obvious: God alone is incomparable. He is incomparable in His being: "Now his being alone is excellent, because there is no such being as his.... He is excellent in all, above all, and beyond all."[23] In addition, God is incomparable in His attributes; that is, "those perfections in the divine nature which are ascribed to him."[24] Finally, God is incomparable in His works: He acts irresistibly ("none can hinder him"), arbitrarily ("according to his own will"), tirelessly ("with ease"), and independently ("without the least help from any other").[25] From this, Swinnock concludes that God is a great God and, therefore, "greatly to be feared."[26] He states, "Between God and us there is an infinite distance, and therefore there ought to be, if it were possible, infinite reverence; he is so vastly above and beyond all others in excellency, that he alone deserves the name of excellency...and he is to be greatly feared."[27]

---

21. Malachi 1:6–14. See Swinnock, *Christian Man's Calling*, 1:184; 2:34; 3:215, 324; *Incomparableness of God*, 4:341; *Door of Salvation*, 5:393, 428.

22. Psalm 89:6.

23. Swinnock, *Incomparableness of God*, 4:387.

24. Swinnock, *Incomparableness of God*, 4:402.

25. Swinnock, *Incomparableness of God*, 4:435–441.

26. Psalm 89:7.

27. Swinnock, *Incomparableness of God*, 4:472.

At this point, Swinnock is careful to distinguish between *filial* and *servile* fear.[28] Servile fear is merely the result of seeing God as a perceived threat. It may cause people to leave their sin for a season, yet it fails to make any lasting impression. In marked contrast, filial fear is an apprehension of the excellence of God's glory, resulting in the proper ordering of the soul's affections: love, desire, delight, fear, sorrow, and hatred.[29]

The Fear of God and the Will

Perceiving God to be "the sweetest love, the richest mercy, the surest friend, the chiefest good, the greatest beauty, the highest honour, and the fullest happiness,"[30] the soul makes Him the object of its love.[31] Swinnock affirms that the mind embraces Him who is "eternal truth" and the will embraces Him

---

28. Swinnock, *Christian Man's Calling*, 3:295.

29. Augustine affirms that desire and joy are the "volition of consent" toward a loved object whereas fear and sorrow are the "volition of aversion" toward a hated object. If an individual's love is "well-directed," then the affections are good. *The City of God*, 14:5–9. He summarizes, "The citizens of the holy city of God, as they live by God's standards in the pilgrimage of this present life, feel fear and desire, pain and gladness in conformity with the holy Scriptures and sound doctrine; and because their love is right, all these affections are right in them." *The City of God*, 14:9. *Augustine: Concerning the City of God against the Pagans*, trans. Henry Bettenson; (Harmondsworth: Penguin Books, 1972), 561.

30. Swinnock, *The Fading of the Flesh and Flourishing of the Faith; or, One Cast for Eternity*, 4:28.

31. For Swinnock, it is impossible to love God without fearing Him. This appears to contradict 1 John 4:18 "There is no fear in love; but perfect love casteth out fear: because fear hath torment." However, Swinnock would argue that this verse refers to servile fear.

who is "infinitely good."[32] Therefore, God (i.e., the eternal truth and infinite good) draws out the greatest love from the soul. For Swinnock, this love focuses entirely upon God, not any perceived benefit derived from Him. To those who profess love for God simply out of self-interest, Swinnock quotes Augustine: "That love is adulterous, and the love of a harlot, which is greater to the gift than the giver."[33] For Swinnock, "nothing which God giveth a godly man will satisfy him, unless God giveth himself to him."[34]

Expectedly, this love cultivates desire: the first "act of love."[35] Swinnock affirms that God must have "incomparable desires, panting, longing, yea, fainting." If there is no "eagerness and earnestness," then there is no love for God. He adds, "The Christian, who hath the blessed God for his portion, strives and labours…and thinks no time too much, no pains too great, no cost enough for the enjoyment of his God."[36] With Matthew 5:6 in mind,[37] Swinnock explains, "a Christian is described by his hungering and thirsting, his panting and breathing after a perfect conformity to God that thereby he may be prepared for perfect communion with God."[38] The only thing that prevents the soul's uninhibited enjoyment of God

---

32. Swinnock, *Fading of the Flesh*, 4:37.

33. Swinnock, *Christian Man's Calling*, 2:64.

34. Swinnock, *Christian Man's Calling*, 3:249.

35. Swinnock, *Incomparableness of God*, 4:475.

36. Swinnock, *Fading of the Flesh*, 4:25.

37. "Blessed are they which do hunger and thirst after righteousness: for they shall be filled."

38. Swinnock, *Christian Man's Calling*, 3:250.

is sin. Recognizing this, the soul hungers and thirsts for righteousness.

The second "act of love" is delight. Quite simply, the soul is "ecstasied in the presence and enjoyment of God."[39] Swinnock sees this *spiritual ecstasy* portrayed in the marriage relationship, commenting, "The love betwixt Christ and his spouse, which is so fervent that she is sick of love to him, and he died for love to her is set out by the love betwixt husband and wife, to shew how great this love is."[40] By virtue of its union with Christ, the soul experiences all that is good and true in God. This delight is not caused by any prospect of reward, but by an admiration of God's glory. Furthermore, it manifests itself in putting "forth more force" in communing with God. Swinnock challenges his readers: "Speak thyself, whether thou prayest, readest, hearest, singest…from love to the infinitely amiable God, from the delight thou takest in communion with him in duties."[41]

Having embraced God as the object of its love, the soul's primary fear is any "approaching evil" that will disrupt its delight in Him. This means the soul fears sin above all else. For Swinnock, this is not a fear of sin's consequences. He explains, "Like the burnt child thou mayest dread the fire of sin, not because it soots and blacks thee, but because it scorches and burns thee."[42] In avoiding sin, many are motivated by the fear of suffering. This reveals that, although sin

---

39. Swinnock, *Incomparableness of God*, 4:475.

40. Swinnock, *Christian Man's Calling*, 1:471–472.

41. Swinnock, *Christian Man's Calling*, 3:295.

42. Swinnock, *Door of Salvation*, 5:69.

is avoided, it is still loved. It also reveals that there is no true appreciation of God's majesty. Swinnock remarks, "To fear sin, as it bringeth a heavy rod, usually proceeds from nature; but to fear sin, as it is a wandering from a holy rule, can proceed only from grace."[43] True fear is exemplified in Joseph's cry, "How then can I do this great wickedness, and sin against God?"[44]

When the soul does experience that which it fears (i.e., sin), there is sorrow which "springeth from the consideration that thou hast sinned against so good, so pure, so perfect a God, in conformity to whom, and communion with whom, all thy happiness consisteth."[45] The unregenerate never experience this because they never feel the burden of their sin as committed against a glorious God. They have not embraced God as the "cream of their affections;" therefore, their heart never breaks because of their sin. In marked contrast, the regenerate experience "evangelical" humiliation: that is, "mourning for sin" and "turning from sin."[46] Swinnock comments, "The Christian who hath truly repented is so sensible of the weight of sin and wrath of God, that he is resolved never more to meddle with those burning coals."[47]

Finally, this "right knowledge" that "falls down upon the heart" results in the proper ordering of hatred. Swinnock explains, "They who know the

---

43. Swinnock, *Door of Salvation*, 5:69–70.

44. Genesis 39:9.

45. Swinnock, *Christian Man's Calling*, 3:341.

46. Swinnock, *Christian Man's Calling*, 1:187.

47. Swinnock, *Christian Man's Calling,* 1:189.

holiness of God...know that sin is loathsome to him, because contrary to his holy nature, and therefore they hate it."[48] Again, "He only hath hateful thoughts of sin...who hath seen the great and glorious, the good and gracious God."[49] The knowledge of God impresses upon the soul the severity of sin. The ensuing hatred leads believers to mortify sin wherever it is found.

The Expression of Swinnock's Piety

In this way, then, the fear of God embraces the whole man: mind and will (i.e., affections and choice). This restoration of the proper functioning of the soul's faculties is pivotal to understand Swinnock's piety.

Believing that the fear of God involves the renewing of the soul's affections, Swinnock states, "They which know experimentally what the sanctification of the Holy Ghost meaneth, are few indeed."[50] By regeneration, the affections embrace God as the greatest good. The soul's love is set upon God. As a result, it desires God and delights in God. Conversely, the soul's hatred is set upon sin. As a result, it fears sin and sorrows for sin. This is at the heart of Swinnock's piety: the conviction that people must experience an affective appropriation of grace.

Believing that the fear of God makes a divorce between sin and the soul, Swinnock seeks to cleanse himself "from all filthiness of the flesh and spirit,

48. Swinnock, *Christian Man's Caling,* 3:155.
49. Swinnock, *Incomparableness of God*, 4:377.
50. Swinnock, *Christian Man's Calling*, 3:205.

perfecting holiness in the fear of God."[51] When the soul embraces God as the greatest good, it hates sin because it is hostile to God. This conviction provides the necessary impetus for mortification. For Swinnock, therefore, the Christian's "great care is every day to conquer his corruptions.... His great end and endeavour, in every providence and every ordinance, is, not the repression, but the ruin of this evil of sin."[52]

Believing that the fear of God is manifested in obedience, Swinnock applies the Bible to all of life, writing, "Whether a Christian be eating or drinking, or buying or selling, or ploughing or sowing, or riding or walking, whatever he be doing, or wherever he be going, he must be always in the fear of the Lord. Godliness must be his guide, his measure, and his end.... Every moment must be devoted to God; and as all seasons, so all actions must be sacred."[53] Simply put, the individual, who delights in God, delights in God's law.

Believing that the fear of God moderates "ill-directed" affections, Swinnock seeks to exercise moderation in all of life. He fears idolatry: the substitution of self for God as the soul's satisfaction. This danger exists in relation to every area of life. Related to this, Swinnock is aware that, in the regenerate, the affections are caught between the sensitive and rational appetites as the image of God is restored. In this condition, his goal is "self-mastery"—the moderation of the sensitive appetite.

---

51. 2 Corinthians 7:1.

52. Swinnock, *Door of Salvation*, 5:97.

53. Swinnock, *Christian Man's Calling*, 1:85.

St. Nicholas in Great Kimble, Buckinghamshire, from which he was ejected for nonconformity in 1662.

(Photograph: Mrs. Sylvia Fox, www.foxyislandwalks.co.uk/)

Believing that the fear of God is cultivated through means, Swinnock exercises himself "unto godliness,"[54] applying himself to "secret, private, and public duties." He views praying, reading and hearing God's Word, and receiving the Lord's Supper as "conduit-pipes" whereby the Holy Spirit stirs the affections;[55] particularly, on the Sabbath—"the market-day for the soul."[56] For Swinnock, the soul that delights in God will delight in the means that lead to God.

Believing that the fear of God "is seminally in the knowledge of God, and floweth from it,"[57] Swinnock devotes himself to a life of structured meditation: "a serious applying [of] the mind to some sacred subject, till the affections be warmed and quickened, and the resolution heightened and strengthened thereby, against what is evil, and for that which is good."[58] As the mind meditates upon God's majesty, sin's severity, Christ's beauty, and the four last things,[59] the Holy Spirit works upon the affections. Love is stirred toward the greatest good (i.e., God) and hatred is stirred toward the greatest evil (i.e., sin). The remaining affections follow accordingly. This stirring of the affections is manifested in a greater resolve against sin.

---

54. 1·Timothy 4:7.

55. Swinnock, *Christian Man's Calling*, 1:102.

56. Swinnock, *Christian Man's Calling*, 1:226.

57. Swinnock, *Christian Man's Calling*, 3:154.

58. Swinnock, *Christian Man's Calling*, 2:425.

59. The "four last things" are death, judgment, hell, and heaven.

Samples of Swinnock's Piety

In the pages that follow, I have included citations from Swinnock that best exemplify his piety as described above. These are organized according to seven sections: (1) the foundation of godliness; (2) the door to godliness; (3) the value of godliness; (4) the pursuit of godliness; (5) the nature of godliness; (6) the means to godliness; and (7) the motives to godliness.

It is my prayer that what follows will lead you to a deeper appreciation for Swinnock's piety. More importantly, it is my prayer (as undoubtedly it would be his) that what follows might contribute in some way to you walking "in the fear of the LORD all the day long."[60]

---

60. Proverbs 23:17.

SECTION ONE

The Foundation
of Godliness

1

The Excellency of the Knowledge of God[1]

If knowledge be the excellency of a man, and differenceth him from a beast, surely then divine knowledge, or the knowledge of God in Christ, is the excellency of a Christian, and differenceth him from other men. Our awe of, love to, and trust in the divine Majesty, are founded in the right knowledge of him. Creatures, the more they are known, the less they are esteemed; but the more the blessed God is known, the more he is prized, desired, and obeyed.[2] Our hatred of sin and contempt of the world proceed from our acquaintance with God. He only hath hateful thoughts of sin, and self-loathing apprehensions because of it, who hath seen the great and glorious, the good and gracious God, whose authority is condemned, whose law is violated, whose name is dishonoured, whose image is defaced, and whose love is abused by it.[3] He only lives above this present evil world, and all the riches and honours and pleasures thereof, who can look beyond it to the infinite God, and those unsearchable riches and weights of glory, and rivers of pleasures that are

---

1. Swinnock, *Incomparableness of God*, 4:377.

2. Psalm 9:10; 73:25; 76:7; 90:11.

3. Job 42:6; Isaiah 6:5.

in and with him. That which was rich and glorious and pleasant to a soul before, hath now no worth, no glory, no pleasure, by reason of that wealth and glory and pleasure which doth so infinitely exceed. When the God of glory appeared to Abraham, he quickly and quietly left his country and kindred, and followed God, not knowing whither he went.[4] If the God of glory appear to your souls, you will soon wink upon these withering vanities, broken cisterns, and gilded nothings, and count them all but dung and dross, for the excellency of the knowledge of him in Christ.

---

4. Genesis 12:1–2; Acts 7:3.

2

⇒⊸•⊶⇐

God is Incomparable in
His Being: Part I[1]

The doctrine which I shall raise out of the words is this,[2] That God is incomparable; or, there is none among the highest, the holiest, in heaven or earth, like unto Jehovah. Take the greatest, the most excellent of beings in this or the other world, yet they come infinitely short of this being of beings: "Among the gods there is none like unto thee, O Lord."[3] Mark, the psalmist doth not choose a weak adversary for God to contend with and conquer, but the strongest. He doth not compare God with the meanest and lowest, but even with the highest, and prefers God before them.... Now his being alone is excellent,[4] because there is no such being as his; there is no being excellent besides his, because there is no being excellent like his. He is excellent in all, above all, and beyond all....

His being is from himself. No being in the world, beside his, is its own cause or original. Angels, men, the highest, yea, the lowest creatures, are derivative

---

1. Swinnock, *Incomparableness of God,* 4:385, 388–392.

2. Swinnock is expounding Psalm 89:6, "For who in the heaven can be compared unto the LORD? Who among the sons of the mighty can be likened unto the LORD?"

3. Psalm 86:8.

4. Job 13:11; Psalm 148:13.

beings. They have what they are from another, even from God. They are drops that flow from the ocean of all beings; they are rays derived from the sun, the fountain of light and entity. The apostle tells us that men are beholden to God for their beings.[5] In him we have our beings…. But God is beholden to none for his being; he was when none else was, even from eternity….[6]

His being is for himself; as he is his own first cause, so he is his own last end; as he is wholly from himself, so he is wholly for himself. All other beings are not of themselves, but for another. "All things were created by him and for him."[7] Since all are from God, it is but reason that all should be for God….[8] It is the excellency and purity of saints and angels to be what they are, and to do what they do, for God, to make him who is the efficient, the final cause of their beings and actions; but it is the excellency of God and purity of God to be what he is, and to do what he doth, for himself. He who is his own happiness must be his own end.

His being is an independent being; he is by himself, as well as from and for himself; none ever in heaven or earth contributed the least towards the maintenance or continuance of his being; neither the creature's goodness nor their goods do him the least good…. He challengeth all the world to produce any being that ever obliged or engaged him in the least:

---

5. Acts 17:28.
6. Psalm 90:1.
7. Colossians 1:16.
8. Romans 14:7.

"Who hath prevented me that I may repay him?"[9] Where is the man, where is the angel, where is the creature that can say, he ever did me the least kindness, that hath been beforehand with me in courtesy, to whom I am the least in debt for my subsistence? I am here ready to make amends; "Who hath prevented me that I may repay him?"

He is an absolutely perfect being.... A being is absolutely perfect when nothing can be added to it, or taken from it, when it is incapable of the least accession or diminution. Now such a being is God, and none but God. As the sun gets nothing by the shining of the moon and the stars, neither loseth anything by their eclipses or withdrawings; so the self-sufficient God gains nothing by all the suits and services, prayers and praises of his creatures; neither loseth anything by their neglect of their duties....

He is an universal being, he hath all good eminently and virtually in himself. Whatsoever excellencies are scattered and dispersed among the creatures in heaven or in earth, they are all united in, and centred after an infinite manner in the Creator. It is a true rule in philosophy, Whatsoever good is in the effect, is more abundantly in the cause. Now God being the principle and cause of all the good and excellency that is in every creature, it must of necessity be more abundantly in him.... The truth is, all the good, all the excellencies that are in men and angels, are not worthy to be a shadow, or foil to set off those excellencies that are in God. All good is in one God....[10]

---

9. Job 41:11.
10. Mark 10:29–30.

3

God is Incomparable in His Being: Part II[1]

God is an unchangeable being, not only without, but incapable of the least alteration. He is the same yesterday, today, and for ever.[2] He is what he was, and what he will be eternally. He is the same since the world was made that he was before the world, and that he will be when this world shall be no more: "With him is not the least variation, or shadow of turning."[3] No variableness. It is an astronomical word, taken from the heavenly bodies, which suffer many declensions and revolutions, which they call parallaxes. Though those heavenly lights are variable, have their increases and decreases, their times of rising and setting; yet our Father of lights is not variable. He knoweth no rising or setting, no increasing or decreasing; but shineth always with the same light and lustre, with the same beauty and brightness....

God is an eternal being, and none is eternal but he.... God hath no succession in his duration; he dwelleth in one indivisible point of eternity; he is what he is in one infinite moment of being; his dura-

---

1. Swinnock, *Incomparableness of God*, 4:393–395, 397–399, 402.
2. Hebrews 13:8.
3. James 1:17.

tion knoweth nothing of former or latter, past or to come; his essence is not bounded by those hedges, but he enjoyeth his whole eternity every moment; hence he is said to "inhabit eternity," to be fixed always in eternity....[4]

God is a simple being. In this I take simplicity, not as opposed to wisdom, for in him are all the treasures of wisdom and knowledge,[5] but as simplicity is opposed to mixture and composition.... So anything, the more simple it is, the more excellent it is. God is a most pure, simple, unmixed, indivisible essence; he is incapable of the least composition, and therefore of the least division. He is one most pure, one without all parts, members, accidents, and qualities. Whatsoever is in him is himself his very being.... God is all essence, all being, and nothing else....

God is an infinite being. He is a being that knoweth no bounds, no limits. His being is without all measure, all degrees and determinations. His understanding, i.e., himself, who is all understanding, is infinite.[6] God is a sphere, whose centre is everywhere, and whose circumference is nowhere. "Behold the heavens, and heaven of heavens cannot contain thee, how much less this house which I have built."[7] The starry heavens, or firmament, is large; it compasseth the whole earth and ocean; this terrestrial world is but a point to it; but the heaven of heavens, or the imperial heaven, is larger; it containeth the lower heaven,

---

4. Isaiah 57:15.

5. Colossians 2:9.

6. Psalm 147:5.

7. 1 Kings 8:27.

but cannot contain the God of heaven.... He is above place, without place, yet in all places....

God is an incomprehensible being, such a being as no creature, whether man or angel, can comprehend or perfectly understand. This floweth from the former; if he be infinite, he must of necessity be incomprehensible; for a finite being, as all are beside himself, can never comprehend what is infinite. There is no proportion between a boundless being and a bounded understanding.... This only can be known of God, that he can never be known fully; and this only can be comprehended of him, that he cannot be comprehended: "Canst thou by searching find out God? canst thou find the Almighty to perfection? It is as high as heaven, what canst thou do? deeper than hell, what canst thou know? The measure thereof is longer than the earth, and broader than the sea."[8]

---

8. Job 11:8–9.

4

—▪●▪—

God is Incomparable in His Attributes[1]

God is incomparable, as in his being, so in his attributes. The attributes of God are those perfections in the divine nature which are ascribed to him, that we might the better understand him. They are so called, i.e., attributes, because they are attributed to him for our sakes, though they are not in him as they are in men and angels....

God is incomparable in his holiness. Holiness in general is the moral goodness of a thing, or its conveniency or agreement with its rule. Holiness in the creatures is their conformity to the will of their Creator in the principle, rule, and end of their actions and motions. Holiness in God is that excellency of the divine nature by which he acteth from himself, for himself, and according to his own will....

God is incomparable in his wisdom.... Wisdom in general is a right understanding of things, and the ordering ourselves and actions suitable to that understanding.... God doth so far exceed angels and men in wisdom that he is said only to be wise: "To the only

---

1. Swinnock, *Incomparableness of God*, 4:402–403, 405–407, 410, 412, 415–417, 419, 423.

wise God;"[2] "To God only wise."[3] None are wise beside him, because none are wise to him.[4] Wisdom is his, his peculiar, his prerogative, his wholly, his only; so his that it is none's but his....

God is incomparable in his power. Power is that ability or force by which we act. Power in God is that attribute by which he effecteth whatsoever he pleaseth. In this he hath no equal: "Who is a strong God like unto thee?"[5] Where is the being that is like him in strength? God is not only strong, but mighty in strength;[6] not only powerful, but excellent in power....[7]

God is incomparable in his justice. Justice in general is the giving every one their due. In God, it is that attribute whereby he disposeth all things according to the rule of equity;[8] and rendereth to every man according to his works, without respect of persons....[9] He is most just, just in the highest degree, just beyond all degrees. He giveth to all their due, without fear of evil—he standeth in awe of none for their power or greatness....

God is incomparable in his knowledge. Knowledge is that attribute of God, whereby he understandeth all things in and of himself.... God knoweth all things from everlasting, before ever the world had a being.

---

2. 1 Timothy 1:17.

3. Romans 16:27.

4. Daniel 5:20.

5. Psalm 89:8.

6. Job 9:4.

7. Job 37:23.

8. Deuteronomy 32:4; Psalm 11:5.

9. Job 34:11, 19; Psalm 62:12; Galatians 6:6–7.

Men and angels may know what is, when it is, but cannot know it as God doth, before it was: "Known to God are all his works, from the beginning of the world."[10] Before he erected the curious frame of the world, he knew all the room and furniture in it, all the motions and actions of all the inhabitants of it. He doth by one pure, simple, undivided, eternal act of his understanding, know all things perfectly, immediately, distinctly, every moment....

God is incomparable in his truth and faithfulness. Truth is that attribute in God whereby he is in himself, as he reveals himself to be, and in his sayings and doings, as he speaketh and acteth....

God is incomparable in his mercy. Mercy is an attribute of God, whereby he pitieth and relieveth his creature in misery. It is an attribute which relateth to the creature only; God knoweth himself, and loveth himself, and glorifieth himself; but he is not merciful to himself. It is an attribute that relateth to the creature in misery.... Fallen man is the proper object of mercy, as being not only undeserving of the least good, but as also having plunged himself into all evil....

God is incomparable in his patience. Patience is that attribute in God whereby he beareth with sinners, and forbears or defers their punishment, or that whereby he expecteth and waiteth long for their conversion. He is a God slow to anger.[11] He waiteth on men to do the good.[12] He is long-suffering.[13] Nay,

---

10. Acts 15:18.
11. Psalm 103:8.
12. Isaiah 30:18.
13. 2 Peter 3:7, 9.

he endureth with much long-suffering the vessels of wrath.[14] He is the God of patience.[15]

These attributes are the very essence of God, not qualities or properties, as in men and angels.... A man may be a man, and not powerful, nor patient, nor merciful; and the reason is, because these properties are really distinct from the essences of man or angels; but in God they are his very being and essence; they are himself, and can no way be separated from him, no more than he can be separated from himself.

---

14. Romans 9:22.
15. Romans 15:5.

5

God is Incomparable in His Works[1]

God is incomparable in his works, as well as in his being and attributes: none hath such a strong hand, such a stretched out arm, or can do like him. "O Lord," saith Moses, "thou hast begun to shew to thy servant thy greatness, and thy mighty hand: for what God is there in heaven or on earth, that can do according to thy works?"[2] He is a God doing wonders....[3]

He is incomparable [in the work of creation].... A goldsmith may make a sparkling jewel, but then you must give him gold and precious stones to make it of; he can put the matter into a better form, but he is so far from making matter where there is none, that he cannot mend the matter which you give him: he cannot make gold of silver, nor diamonds of common stones. Man's work may exceed the matter, but man's work cannot make the matter exceed itself. But God can not only make the matter to exceed itself,—as in man, who is formed of the dust of the earth, he hath such curious parts, veins, sinews, arteries, &c.; such members, eyes, cheeks, ears, &c.; such characters of beauty on the whole, that he looks nothing like his parent earth, the matter of which he was made,—but

---

1. Swinnock, *Incomparableness of God*, 4:424–428, 432–433.

2. Deuteronomy 3:24.

3. Exodus 15:11.

also make matter: he hath brought something, nay, all things out of nothing. All the angels and men cannot create one grain of corn, one pile of grass, one mote of dust; but the great God hath erected the stately fabric of heaven and the earth, with the curious steps and stories thereof, and the various creatures and furniture therein, of nothing. Hereby he proves himself the true God, "The living God that made heaven and earth, and all things therein."[4]

He is incomparable in regard of providence. (1) For preservation none is like him, nay, none beside him doth this: "O thou preserver of men;"[5] "thy visitation preserveth my spirit."[6] God is unlike to men; the carpenters or masons build houses, and then leave them to the care and charge of others; but God keeps up what he sets up. His providence succeedeth creation, and is indeed a continual creation: "Thou preservest man and beast"....[7] (2) For gubernation; he governeth all, and neither men nor angels can govern themselves. The great family of the world would soon lose its beauty, yea, its being, if he did not maintain its harmony and concord, by guiding them in their motions, keeping them in their several stations, and directing them to their ends: "The Lord hath established his throne in the heavens, and his kingdom ruleth over all"....[8]

---

4. Acts 14:15.
5. Job 2:20.
6. Job 10:12.
7. Psalm 36:6.
8. Psalm 103:19.

Portrayal of a goldsmith's shop in Swinnock's days.

(From the frontispiece in
A Touch-Stone for Gold and Silver Wares [London, 1677])

He is incomparable in the work of redemption. And truly this work is his masterpiece, pure workmanship; and, indeed, all his works of creation and providence are subordinate to this. All his attributes sparkle most gloriously in this;[9] all his angels in heaven admire and adore him for this.[10] This is the work of all his works, which he is so mightily pleased with, and reapeth so much glory and praise from.[11] No angels, no men, no not all together, could with all their united worthiness redeem one soul.... None had pity enough for man's misery.... None had wisdom enough to find out a remedy.... None had power to have gone through with the work.

---

9. Psalm 102:16.

10. Revelation 4:10–11

11. Isaiah 42:1; 43:21.

6

The Reasonableness of Worship[1]

If God be an incomparable God, then incomparable service and worship is due to him. All service must be suitable to its object. The higher the prince, the higher the honour he doth and may expect.... God is a great God, and therefore must have great worship.... It reflects upon God, it is a slighting him, to give him anything that is ordinary, as it is to a king to be put off with common entertainment at the houses of his subjects. As he is the best, so he will be served with the best....

This incomparable God calls for incomparable awe and reverence. Excellency commandeth awe.... The greater distance between any persons, the greater reverence is expected.... But now between God and us there is an infinite distance, and therefore there ought to be, if it were possible, infinite reverence; he is so vastly above and beyond all others in excellency, that he alone deserves the name of excellency, therefore his name is holy and reverend and he is to be greatly feared.[2] The greatest excellency calleth for the greatest reverence....[3]

---

1. Swinnock, *Incomparableness of God,* 4:471–476.

2. Psalm 111:9.

3. Psalm 89:6–7; 96:4; Proverbs 23:17.

This incomparable God calls for incomparable humility and lowliness of spirit from us. The height of God must lay man low, and the matchless excellency of God make him base in his own eyes. When we behold ourselves in the glass of those that have little or nothing that is good or praiseworthy, or that have less than ourselves, then we spread out our plumes, and are puffed up with pride, and judge ourselves comely creatures; but if we would behold ourselves in the glass of the incomparable God, in whose sight the heavens are unclean, in whose presence angels vail their faces, to whom ten thousand suns are perfect darkness, and all the world less than nothing; how should we pluck in our plumes, and abhor ourselves for our pride! Man never comes to a right knowledge of himself, what a pitiful, abominable wretch he is, till he comes to a right knowledge of God, what an excellent incomparable majesty he is....

This incomparable God calls for incomparable love, the top, the cream of our affections. Good is the object of love...the greater therefore the good is, the greater love it requireth; and God being the greatest good, must have the greatest love.... He deserves the greatest extensively, the heart, soul, mind, and strength; the greatest intensively, all the heart, all the soul, all the mind, all the strength.[4] Reader, thy love to him must be so great that thy love to thy father, mother, wife, child, house, land, and life, must be hatred in comparison of it, and in competition with it....[5]

---

4. Matthew 22:37.

5. Luke 14:26.

This incomparable God must have incomparable trust. The more able and faithful any person is, the more firmly we trust him. Now, God is incomparable in power, he hath an almighty arm; incomparable in faithfulness, he cannot lie....[6] Therefore God must have our surest love and firmest faith.[7] We must esteem his words as good as deeds; and rely on all he promiseth as if it were already performed. We must not stagger or waver, but "draw nigh to him with full assurance of faith"....[8]

This incomparable God must have incomparable obedience in the course of our lives. The more virtuous, or gracious, or honourable, or excellent, the person is with whom we walk, the more we weigh our words, and ponder the paths of our feet, and watch over ourselves. God is incomparable in purity, in jealousy, in majesty, in excellency; therefore they who are ever under his eye and in his presence, and who walk with him, must walk, not as they do when with ordinary persons, carelessly and negligently, but circumspectly, accurately, exactly, to a hair's-breadth, as on a ridge.[9]

---

6. Titus 1:2; Hebrews 6:18.
7. Romans 4:20.
8. Hebrews 10:22.
9. Ephesians 5:15.

7

The Sinfulness of Sin[1]

If God be so incomparable, that there is none on earth, none in heaven comparable to him, it may inform us of the great venom and malignity of sin, because it is an injury to so great, so glorious, so incomparable a being. The higher and better any object is, the baser and the worse is that action which is injurious to it. To throw dirt on sackcloth is not so bad as to throw dirt on scarlet or fine linen. To make a flaw in a pebble of common stone is nothing to the making a flaw in a diamond of precious stone. Those opprobrious speeches, or injurious actions, against an ordinary person, which are but a breach of the good behaviour, and bear but a common action at law, if against a prince, may be high treason, because of the excellency of his place, and majesty of his person. The worth and dignity of the object doth exceedingly heighten and aggravate the offence. How horrid then is sin, and of how heinous a nature, when it offendeth and opposeth not kings, the highest of men, not angels, the highest of creatures, but God, the highest of beings; the incomparable God, to whom kings and angels, yea, the whole creation is less than nothing! We take the size of sin too low, and short, and wrong, when we measure it by the wrong it doth to ourselves,

---

1. Swinnock, *Incomparableness of God*, 4:456–460.

or our families, or our neighbours, or the nation wherein we live; indeed, herein somewhat of its evil and mischief doth appear; but to take its full length and proportion, we must consider the wrong it doth to this great, this glorious, this incomparable God. Sin is incomparably malignant, because the God principally injured by it is incomparably excellent....

This, this is the only glass that discovers the horrid ugly features, the monstrous frightful deformities of sin's face, that it is a wrong to the blessed God, to him who is the high and lofty One.[2]

1. In that sin is a breach of this incomparable God's law, a violation of his command, a contradiction of his will: "Whosoever sinneth transgresseth the law, for sin is a transgression of the law."[3] Neither the greatness nor smallness of our obedience or disobedience is to be valued according to the greatness or smallness of the thing commanded or forbidden, not according to the greatness or smallness of the good or hurt done to man by it, but according to the greatness of the person who commandeth or forbiddeth.

2. In that it is a contempt of this incomparable God's authority, a slighting his dominion, a denying his sovereignty: "Who is the Lord, that I should obey his voice?"[4] is the voice of every sinner. "We are our own, say they; who is Lord over us?"[5] They know no maker, and therefore own no master. For this cause

2. Isaiah 57:15.

3. 1 John 3:4.

4. Exodus 5:2.

5. Psalm 12:4.

the sinner is said to cast the incomparable God behind his back, as not worth minding or regarding.[6]

3. In that it is a dishonouring this incomparable God, whose name alone is excellent.... Sin layeth the honour of this incomparable God, which is more worth than millions of worlds, in the dust, and trampleth on it...it disgraceth his justice, thence is called unrighteousness;[7] his wisdom, thence is called folly;[8] his patience, thence is called murmuring;[9] his power, thence is called weakness;[10] his mercy, thence is called unthankfulness;[11] his knowledge, thence is called ignorance, and a work of darkness;[12] his truth, thence is called a lie and lying vanity.[13] In all these, and every way, it disgraceth his holiness, which is his glory, and the glory of all his attributes,[14] thence is called filthiness;[15] uncleanness.[16]

4. In that it is a fighting with, and to its power, a destroying this incomparable God. The murder of any man is heinous, it is horrid, it is against nature, and it is the extremist mischief that one creature can do to another.[17] The murder of a father or a sovereign

---

6. 1 Kings 14:9.
7. 1 John 1:6.
8. Proverbs 5:23.
9. Jude 1:16.
10. Romans 5:8.
11. Luke 6:35.
12. Ephesians 5:8; 1 Peter 1:14.
13. Psalm 58:2; Jonah 2:8.
14. Exodus 15:11.
15. 2 Corinthians 7:1.
16. Romans 1:24.
17. Genesis 4:10; Matthew 10:28.

is far more heinous, as being more against nature, and against more engagements to the contrary. He is cursed that mocketh his father, and his heart smote him who did but cut off the skirt of his king's garment,[18] though his enemy; what a monster then is he that kills either! but, oh, what a monster, what a devil is that which destroyeth, as far as it is able, the good, the gracious, the great, the glorious, the incomparable God! Truly, sin is such a monster, such a devil, that were its power equal to its spite, and its strength to its malice, the living God should not live a moment....

Oh how odious, how loathsome, how abominable is sin, that breaks the law, slights the authority, dishonours the name, and to its utmost dethrones and destroys the being of this incomparable God, this self-sufficient, independent, absolutely perfect, eternal, incomprehensible, infinite being, which alone deserves the name of being, and to which all other beings are no beings! Reader, should this God of glory appear to thee, as once to Abraham, and shew thee a glimpse of his excellent glory, that is above the heavens...what wouldst thou then think of sin? Oh, what wouldst thou then think of thyself for thy sins? Shouldst thou not have other thoughts of sin, and of thyself for sin, than ever yet thou hast had? Wouldst thou not even loathe thyself for being so base, so vile, so unworthy, yea, so mad as to offend and affront, and fight against such a God?

---

18. 1 Samuel 24:5.

SECTION TWO

The Door
to Godliness

8

—————— ✦ ——————

The Need for Regeneration[1]

If you ask me what is the chiefest thing in the world for a man to mind; what is that which is worthy of all his time, and strength, and thoughts, and words, and actions? I answer, regeneration. If you demand what is that which is of greatest necessity and excellency, that bringeth in the greatest profit, delight, and happiness? I answer, regeneration. He that hath this, hath all that is worth having; the having of this is heaven. He that wanteth this hath nothing; the whole world cannot make up the want of this; the want of this is hell....

I shall speak to the reasons why there is a necessity of regeneration in every man that would obtain salvation.

First, Because every man must be prepared for, before he can be admitted into, that holy place. We say in philosophy, nature doth nothing *per saltum*;[2] the ground is prepared for an harvest by being dunged, ploughed, and sowed; it is as true in this point of divinity; the God of nature will not save a man *per saltum*, nor remove a swine out of a stye, immediately into a dining-room; nor take a sinner reeking in his lusts, and presently invest him with a crown of life;

---

1. Swinnock, *Door of Salvation*, 5:7, 38–41.

2. I.e., by a leap; by fits and starts.

no, the man must be prepared by regeneration or holiness in part, for salvation or holiness which is perfect. The heathen king would not admit virgins to his bed till they had been purified.[3] And surely the King of kings will not receive any into his nearest and dearest embraces, till they are "cleansed from all pollutions both of flesh and spirit"....

Secondly, Every man must be regenerated or he cannot be saved, because all that attain heaven must be interested in the purchaser of heaven. Those that go to that place must be united to, and have a part in him that laid down the price....[4] There are two changes indispensably requisite in all that would be saved. The one is the change of a man's state, or a moral change, when of a bondman to sin and Satan he is made a freeman,[5] when of a slave to the devil he is made the son of God; when he is brought from under the covenant of works, to be under the covenant of grace; when of an enemy to God he is reconciled to him by the death of his Son; when though he were far off, he is made nigh; though he was not beloved, yet now he is beloved; though he was a child of wrath, is now a vessel of mercy.[6] The other is the change of a man's nature, or a physical change, when the whole man is renewed after the image of God. The former is relative, this is real; the former is the change of his condition, this of his disposition; the former change is wrought in justification, this in regeneration....

---

3. Esther 2:12.

4. Acts 4:12; Hebrews 10:19; 1 John 2:29.

5. John 8:36.

6. John 1:12; Romans 5:10; 9:23; Ephesians 2:3; 1 Peter 2:9–10.

Therefore regeneration is required, because by it the creature is planted into Christ; regeneration cutteth the man off from his own stock and grafteth him into the Lord Jesus; regeneration throweth the sinner off from his own bottom, and builds him on the Saviour as a sure foundation. Regeneration is, as it were, the minister which marrieth Christ and the soul together; therein the soul giveth itself unfeignedly to Christ, and Christ giveth himself really to the soul, and thereby the sins and weaknesses of the soul, the wife's, become the husband's; and the riches, and righteousness, the home and heaven of Christ, the husband's, become the wife's.

9

The Nature of Regeneration[1]

Regeneration is a work of God's Spirit, whereby he doth, out of his mere good pleasure, for his own glory and the salvation of his elect, at first renew the whole man after his own image by the ministry of the word....

First, I call it a work of God's Spirit; here is the efficient principal cause of it. The babe of grace in this respect calleth none on earth father. It is by the Spirit overshadowing the soul that this new creature is conceived and brought forth; godliness is not natural, but adventitious to man; not by propagation, but by donation. Man cannot generate himself naturally, much less regenerate himself spiritually; they which are born of the flesh contribute nothing to their own beings, neither do they which are born of the Spirit bring anything to their new beings, unless it be a passive receptiveness, as they are reasonable creatures....

Secondly, I say, "Whereby God out of his mere good pleasure," here is the impulsive or moving cause of regeneration; "of his own will begat he us again by the word of truth."[2] God's goodwill is the highest moving cause of this gracious work; it was

---

1. Swinnock, *Door of Salvation*, 5:20, 22–27, 34–35.
2. James 1:18.

not any foresight of faith or good works, not anything without him that turned the scale of his thoughts for thy purity and peace, but only his own good pleasure and pity.... If you would know the grand reason why some are taken by the net of the word, let down in the sea of the world, when others are left; why some like wax are melted before this fire of Scripture, when others like clay are hardened; why some have the light side of this glorious pillar towards them, when others have the dark side of it; why the same path of the Red Sea is salvation to some, when it is destruction to others; why the "mysteries of the kingdom of heaven are revealed to babes, when they are hid from the wise and prudent:" I must give you the same reason which Christ himself doth, "Even so, Father, because it seemeth good in thy sight."[3]

Thirdly, here is the instrumental cause. I say, "by the ministry of the word." "Of his own will begat he us again by the word of truth."[4] Scripture is the ordinary means of conversion; "The gospel of Christ is the power of God unto salvation"....[5] "The law of the Lord is perfect, converting the soul."[6] It is the incorruptible seed of the word, which by those spiritual husbandmen is thrown into the soil of men's hearts, that, through the influence of the Sun of righteousness and dews of heaven, springeth up in grace and holiness....

---

3. Matthew 11:27.

4. James 1:18.

5. Romans 1:16.

6. Psalm 19:7.

Fourthly, here is the formal cause of regeneration, whereby God doth at first renew the whole man after his own image; now because this is the cause which doth specially difference a thing, and this being opened, its nature will best appear, I shall speak the more to it, and observe in it these four particulars....

1. For the act, I call it a renewing...[7]upon a double account; partly because in regeneration nature is not ruined, but rectified. The convert is the same man, but new made. The faculties of his soul are not destroyed, but they are refined.... Again, I call it a renewing, partly because of the great change which is wrought in a man converted....

2. The subject; I call it a renewing of the whole man. As in our first birth, not one part or member is born, but every one; so in our second birth the whole man is new born. By our first birth the whole man is polluted, and therefore by our second birth the whole man must be purified. Original sin defileth the whole man, from the crown of the head to the soles of the feet; and regeneration refineth the whole man, soul, body, and spirit....[8] In the new creature, though every part be not throughout sanctified, yet he is sanctified in every part throughout; he hath a perfection of parts, though not of degrees....

3. I observe in this formal cause, the pattern, it is a renewing of the whole man after the image of God. Man's loss and misery by his fall consisteth in these two things: (1) He lost God's image and likeness; (2) God's favour and love. Now that the second Adam

---

7. Ephesians 4:23–24; Titus 3:5.
8. Romans 3:13–14; 1 Thessalonians 5:23.

might recover us to God's love, he doth imprint on us God's image; for likeness is the ground of love. Therefore the regenerate are said to be partakers of the divine nature,[9] and the new man, which they put on in conversion, is said to be after God, and after the image of him that created them;[10] the law of God is written in their hearts;[11] which law is nothing but a conformity or likeness to the nature and will of the Lord. The corrupt image of Satan and the old Adam is defaced; therefore it is called a putting off the old man;[12] the pure image of God is introduced, therefore it is called a putting on the new man;[13] which after God is created in righteousness and true holiness; and a being holy as God is holy.[14] And, indeed, all these new-born children do, so far as they are regenerate, completely resemble their Father. Their godliness is nothing but god-likeness, a beam of the divine glory, a representation of God's own perfections....

4. I observe, in this formal cause, the season. I say it is the work of God's Spirit, whereby he doth at first renew the whole man after his own image. These words *at first* do distinguish regeneration from sanctification. Sanctification is a constant, progressive renewing of the whole man, whereby the new creature doth daily more and more die unto sin and live unto God. Regeneration is the birth, sanctification

---

9. 2 Peter 1:4.

10. Ephesians 4:23; Colossians 3:10.

11. Hebrews 8:10.

12. Ephesians 4:23; Colossians 3:9.

13. Ephesians 4:24.

14. 1 Peter 1:14–16.

is the growth of this babe of grace. In regeneration, the sun of holiness rises; in sanctification it keepeth its course, and shineth brighter and brighter unto the perfect day.[15] The former is a specific change from nature to grace;[16] the latter is a gradual change from one degree of grace to another....

Fifthly, Here is the definition of the final causes of regeneration, the glory of God and the salvation of his elect. The first is the more, the other the less principal end. They are both joined together in God's decree and intention, and in the saints' calling, and the execution of his decree. "The Lord made all things for himself,"[17] but especially the new creation: that being his masterpiece and choice work, is particularly designed for the credit of the workman: "All thy works shall praise thee, O God, and thy saints shall bless thee."[18]

---

15. Proverbs 4:18.
16. Ephesians 5:8.
17. Proverbs 16:3.
18. Psalm 145:10.

10

The Effect of Regeneration[1]

Thou art to understand that conversion is not wrought all together and at once, but by degrees.... The match between Christ and the soul is not huddled up in haste. Christ first goeth a-wooing. The Father offereth a large portion with his Son. The creature considereth his terms: how lovely his person is, what his precepts will be, what advantage he shall have by the marriage; and by a deep and powerful energy of the Spirit, consenteth to take him for his lord and husband.

The first step is illumination. The Spirit of God doth in the first place open the eyes of the blind, and turn men from darkness to light.... Before the Sun of righteousness ariseth on the soul, there is daybreak of light in the understanding....

The second step which the Spirit takes is conviction.[2] The sun, which before did enlighten the mind, doth now slide down with its heating and scorching beams into the conscience. That knowledge which the sinner had of his sins before was speculative but now becomes practical, making sin a lump of lead upon tender flesh, that the conscience is exceedingly pressed and oppressed with it. Conviction is the

---

1. Swinnock, *Door of Salvation,* 5:200–203, 205–209, 211, 213–214, 217.

2. John 16:9–10.

application of the nature of sin, and danger of sinners, to himself in particular, which before he knew in the general.... The Spirit of God convinceth the sinner of four things. (1) The Spirit convinceth him of his great and innumerable corruptions.... Truly this poor sinner, beholding himself in the glass of law, and viewing those hellish spots of sin all over his soul and body, he abhorreth himself in dust and ashes.... (2) The Spirit convinceth him of his miserable and dreadful condition.... He thought before that he was whole, a sound man, to have little need of a physician; but now he both seeth his sores and feeleth his wounds.... Alas, alas! thinks he, I am a dead, a damned man; the almighty God is angry; the weight of my sins at present is heavy; but the sufferings which I am every moment liable to, are infinite and eternal.... (3) The Spirit convinceth him of the impotency and weakness of anything in the world to help him, that in the whole garden of nature there is never an herb which can make a salve to heal his wounded conscience. Now the sinner is scorched with the heat of God's wrath; he is like a man in a burning fever, full of pain, and he tumbleth and tosseth from one side of the bed to the other, trying and hoping for ease; he goeth to this carnal comfort, or that human help, to have his pain abated, and his sores cured; but none of them will do; as fast as he claps on those carnal plasters, the Spirit causeth his conscience to rub them off.... (4) The Spirit convinceth him of the willingness, suitability, and all-sufficiency of Christ to help and heal him.... The sinner now in his burning fit is very thirsty.... When the sinner is brought to this strait, the Spirit of God openeth his eyes to see a well of salvation, even Jesus, who delivereth from the wrath to come....

The third step which the Spirit takes is anhelation,[3] to cause the soul of the convinced sinner to breathe and pant after Jesus Christ. Breath is the first effect of life. Conviction hath emptied his stomach of creature confidence, and self-righteousness made him poor in spirit, and oh how hungry he is after the righteousness of Jesus Christ, the bread which came down from heaven! As the thirsty ground cleaves and opens for drops, as the hart panteth after waterbrooks, so panteth his soul after Jesus Christ, God blessed for ever....

The fourth step is lamentation. The soul that breatheth after a Saviour is truly broken for his sins; his groans after liberty are accompanied with grief for his slavery. Now the clouds gather and thicken over the soul, and fall down in tears; his sorrow under the conviction of his misery was legal, but now it is for his abuse of mercy, and so evangelical. His heart before was as a cloud broken by a thunderbolt, being torn in pieces violently, and making a mighty noise; but now, like the cloud melted by the shining of the sun upon it, it dissolves down sweetly into a fruitful shower. He looked on sin before as it was damning, as that which would cast his soul and body into hell; but now he looks on sin as it is defiling, as that which makes him unlike to God, and as that by which he hath abused love and mercy; and the consideration of this warmeth his heart, and kindly thaweth it....

---

3. I.e., short and rapid breathing.

The fifth step is implantation into Christ; the Spirit now leadeth the child by the hand unto Christ, nay, grafteth him into Christ. The soul being convinced of the necessity it stands in of Christ, of the endless misery which it must undergo without Christ, of the all-sufficiency that is in Christ, how willing, how able he is to bind up the broken heart, and to save the sinful soul, doth by the help of the Holy Ghost venture itself, and its everlasting estate, upon Jesus Christ, resolving to stand or fall, live or die, at his feet....

The last step is a resolution of the sinner to give up himself to all the laws of Christ, or a hearty acceptation of the Redeemer as Saviour and sovereign. The heart of the man is so melted by evangelical sorrow for sin, and the heat of God's love to his soul, that he is soft like wax for any impression; God may command him what he pleaseth; he cleaveth to the law with full purpose of heart. Before, he was like the prodigal, he must go as far as he could from his Father's house; the orders there were too pure, the laws there too strict, the discipline there too severe; he travelleth therefore into a far country. But now the man is hungry...it is his meat and drink to do the will of God.

11

The Marks of Regeneration[1]

The Scripture setteth down the signs of the men and women which are sanctified, and which shall be saved....

First, There is in this new nature a dying to sin. The apostle calleth it a putting off the old man,[2] and a dying to sin....[3] The old man "is crucified." Sin, like an old man in them which are new made doth decay and decline every day; it is every hour growing weaker and weaker and nearer to its grave and utter abolition. Regeneration giveth sin its death's wound, though, as those that are crucified, it dieth lingeringly, yet it dieth certainly. Sin, like a man in consumption, in a converted person is always wasting and dying, till at last it is quite dead. One that is mortally wounded sprawleth and moveth for a time, but afterwards giveth up the ghost; so sin, while saints live, though it be mortally wounded, doth rage and stir, but it abateth in strength, and dieth with them....

The new creature is like unto God, of purer eyes than to behold iniquity.[4] The evil of sin cannot ordinarily get a good look from him; he cannot meet this

---

1. Swinnock, *Door of Salvation*, 5:94–97, 105–108.

2. Ephesians 4:22.

3. Romans 6:11.

4. Habakkuk 1:13.

ugly guest in any corner of his house but his heart
riseth against him; he considereth what a Lord sin
displeaseth, what a law sin transgresseth, what a
beautiful image sin defaceth, what a glorious name
sin dishonoureth, what a lovely, loving Saviour sin
buffeted shamefully and tortured cruelly, what a
precious soul and peerless salvation sin was like to
have lost him eternally. And oh it is a killing look
which this soul giveth his dearest lust! Ah, thinks he,
that ever my nature should hatch and harbour such
hideous monsters! That ever my heart should be a
polluted bed to breed and bring forth such a poison-
ous brood! It was my iniquity that bade defiance
to the highest Majesty; it was my corruption which
scourged the back, wounded the head, nailed the
feet and hands, yea, pierced the very heart of Jesus
Christ; my wickedness was the weight which caused
his bloody sweat; my lust was the murderer which
put to death the Lord of life; it was my covetousness
which betrayed him, my cowardliness which condemned him, and my cruelty which executed him;
and shall I be a friend to that traitor which was a foe
to my Redeemer! Well, whatever it cost me, through
the strength of Christ I will have justice upon these
murderers....

His great care is every day to conquer his corruptions. The body of sin and death, to which he is tied,
is as noisome to his soul as a dead body to his senses.
Lust is as burdensome to him as a withered arm,
which hangs on a man like a lump of lead. Never did
prisoner more ardently desire to be rid of his fetters,
than this saint to be freed from subjection to his sins.
The distressed Jews did not groan so much under

their Egyptian slavery as this true Israelite for spiritual liberty: "O wretched man that I am," saith he, "who shall deliver me from this body of sin and death?"[5] His great end and endeavour, in every providence and every ordinance, is, not the repression, but the ruin of this evil of sin....

Secondly, There is in this new creature, as a dying to sin, so also a living to God in all ways of obedience.[6] As the old man is put off, so the new man is put on; besides the expulsion of sin, there is the infusion of holiness. A habit or principle of grace is bestowed on the soul, whereby it breatheth after, exerciseth and delighteth itself in, the ways and worship of God; there is an inward frame and disposition infused into the new creature, different from, nay, contrary to, his former inclinations: the stream of his heart and life before ran swiftly after the flesh and the world.... But now the tide is turned, the waters run in another channel; the Lord is exalted in his affections, as his chiefest good, and in his conversation[7] as his utmost end.... His will chooseth him, his affections love him, his desire is after him, his delight is in him, his fear is of him, his trust is on him, his care and endeavour is to walk worthy of the Lord unto all well-pleasing....[8]

Now reader, try thyself: art thou alive to God? Dost thou take him in Christ for thy happiness, and make him thine end?.... Hast thou found that it is good

---

5. Romans 7:24.

6. Romans 6:11.

7. I.e., life.

8. Genesis 42:18; Psalm 16:5–6; 37:4; 73:25–26; Isaiah 7:8; John 17:3.

for thee to draw nigh to God?.... Examine thine heart; for if thou hast the divine nature, divine and spiritual things will be natural, and so pleasant to thee.

The Value
of Godliness

12

Our Great End[1]

Now the great end to which man is designed by God, is the exercising himself to godliness. God erected the stately fabric of the great world for man, but he wrought the curious piece of the little world [man] for himself. Of all his visible works he did set man apart for his own worship. Man, saith one, is the end of all in a semicircle, intimating that all things in the world were made for man, and man was made for God....

The great God, according to his infinite wisdom, hath designed all his creatures to some particular ends, and hath imprinted in their natures an appetite and propensity towards that end, as the point and scope of their being. Yea, the very inanimate and irrational creatures are serviceable to those ends and uses in their several places and stations.... Surely much more is man, the point in which all those lines meet, designed to some noble end, suitable to the excellency of his being; and what can that be, but to worship the glorious and blessed God, and the exercising himself to godliness?

"The Lord made all things for himself."[2] God made things without life and reason to serve him passively and subjectively, by administering occasion

---

1. Swinnock, *Christian Man's Calling*, 1:47–49.
2. Proverbs 16:4.

to man to admire and adore his Maker; but man was made to worship him actively and affectionately, as sensible of, and affected with, that divine wisdom, power, and goodness which appear in them. As all things are of him as the efficient cause, so all things must necessarily be for him as the final cause. But man in an especial manner is predestinated and created for this purpose: "Thou art mine; I have created him for my glory; I have formed him, yea, I have made him."[3] There is both the author and the end of our creation: the author, "I have created him;" the end, "for my glory"....

Man is made as a glass, to represent the perfections that are in God. A glass can receive the beams of the sun into it, and reflect them back again to the sun. The excellencies of God appear abundantly in his works; man is made to be the glass where these beams of divine glory should be united and received, and also from him reflected back to God again.

---

3. Isaiah 43:1, 7.

13

Our Great Weight[1]

Godliness ought to be every man's main business, because it is a work of the greatest concernment and weight. Things that are of most stress call for our greatest strength. Our utmost pains ought to be laid out upon that which is of highest price: man's diligence about any work must be answerable to the consequence of the work. The folly of man seldom appears more than in being very busy about nothing....

Now godliness is, amongst all man's works, of the greatest weight. The truth is, he hath no work of weight but this; this is the one thing necessary, and in this one thing are man's all things. Our unchangeable weal or woe in the other world is wrapped up in our diligence or negligence about this; our earthly business, be they about food or raiment, about honours or pleasures, or whatsoever, are but toys and trifles, but baubles and butterflies, to this. As candles before the sun, they must all disappear and give place to this....

We may say of this work of Christianity, compared with all other works, what David said of Goliath's sword, "There is none like it;"[2] this is soul-work, this is God-work, this is eternity-work, and therefore of greatest weight, and requireth us all to make it our

---

1. Swinnock, *Christian Man's Calling*, 1:50–58.
2. 1 Samuel 21:9.

business; such blows as these three are, one would think, might force fire out of flint.

This is soul-work: as soul-woe is the heaviest woe, and soul-wants are the greatest wants, so soul-work is the weightiest work; the dangers of a soul are the deepest dangers, the loss of the soul is the dreadfullest loss, the neglect of the soul is the dolefullest neglect. The consequence of the action is frequently specified from the excellency of the person or subject concerned in it. The soul of man is a most excellent piece, both in regard of the spirituality and immortality of its substance, as also in regard of that divine image imprinted on it, those heavenly qualities with which it was at first endowed.... Godliness must therefore be followed with care and conscience....

Godliness, as it is soul-work, so it is God-work; as the excellency of the subject in which, so also the excellency of the object about which, it is conversant, speaks it to be weighty.... When we deal with our equals, with them that stand upon the same level with us, we may deal as men; our affections may be like scales that are evenly poised, in regard of indifference, but when we have to do with a God so great, that in comparison of him the vast ocean, the broad earth, and the highest heavens are all less than nothing, and so glorious that the greatest lights of the world, though every star were a sun, yet in respect of him are perfect darkness, we must be like angels, our affections should be all in a flame in regard of fervency and activity....

Further, godliness is eternity-work, and therefore must needs be of infinite weight, and is worthy of all our pains and diligence.... Eternal life is promised to the diligent, eternal death is the portion of the negligent. The former shall be bathed in "the rivers of God's eternal pleasures,"[3] the latter shall suffer the "vengeance of eternal fire."[4] To be tormented day and night for ever and ever, and to enjoy the "exceeding and eternal weight of glory,"[5] are certainly no jesting matters, but of more concernment than we can possibly conceive. Who would not labour hard to attain eternal life! Who would not work night and day to avoid eternal death, eternal woe!

---

3. Psalm 36:8.

4. Jude 7.

5. 2 Corinthians 4:17.

14

Our Great Reward[1]

Godliness must be made our principal business, our main work, because otherwise we shall lose our reward.... The reward of godliness is of infinite worth, the end of holiness (as of hope) is the salvation of the soul, the eternal immediate enjoyment of God in heaven. Now, who can think to attain the place of such ravishing pleasures without much pains?

Nature herself will not bestow her precious treasure without much unwearied labour.... When did we ever find nature so prodigal of her gifts, as to bestow skill and excellency in any art or science, without industry and diligence? Doth she not force her students to beat their brains, to waste their bodies, to break their sleep, to burn up their strength, before she will permit them to pry into her secrets, to pick the lock of her curious cabinet, and gain any considerable knowledge of her wealth and richness? And can we think the God of nature will give men to know him, as they are known of him—will bestow on them the unspeakable gift, the pearl of price, the Holy of holies, such things as eye hath not seen, nor ear heard, neither man's heart conceived, while they lie lazying on the bed of idleness?

---

1. Swinnock, *Christian Man's Calling*, 1:59–60, 65–66.

Statue of Henry IV of France (1589–1610),
cast in 1818 by François-Frédéric Lamot

The French Duke d'Alva could say, when he was asked by Henry the Fourth[2] whether he had seen the eclipse of the sun, that he had so much business to do upon earth, that he had no time to look up to heaven. Sure I am, the Christian may say with more truth and conscience, that he hath so much business to do for heaven, that he hath no time to mind vain or earthly things. That servant who doth ponder the strictness of his master, consider the shortness of his time, conceive the largeness of his task, and believe the weightiness of his work, how it must be done, or he is undone for ever, will be easily convinced that it very nearly concerns him, that it highly behoves him, to shake off sloth and sluggishness, to gird up the loins of his mind, to give it the precedency in all his actions, to pursue it with industry against all opposition, to persevere in it with constancy to his dissolution, and, in a word, to make it his main business, his principal work.

---

2. This is likely a reference to Henry IV of France (1589–1610). In 1598, he enacted the Edict of Nantes, granting religious liberty to Protestants.

The Pursuit of Godliness

15

Godliness must have Precedency[1]

For a man to exercise himself to godliness.. [is] to give it the precedency in all our actions. That which a man maketh his business, he will be sure to mind, whatsoever he omits. A good husband will serve his shop before his sports, and will sometimes offer a handsome and warrantable kind of disrespect to his friends, that his calling may have his company.... He that makes religion his business, carrieth himself towards his general, as this man doth towards his particular, calling. In his whole life he walks with God, and is so mannerly and dutiful, as to give God the upper hand all the way. He knoweth that his God must be worshipped, that his family must be served, and that his calling must be followed, (for religion doth not nullify, only rectify his carriage towards his earthly vocation;) but each in their order,—that which is first in regard of excellency is first in regard of his industry. He is not so unnatural as to serve his cattle before his children, nor so atheistical as to serve his body and the world before his soul and his Saviour. He is so sensible of his infinite engagements to the blessed God, that he allotteth some time every day for his religious duties....

---

1. Swinnock, *Christian Man's Calling*, 1:36–37.

He that minds religion by the by, will, if other things intervene, put it back, and be glad of an excuse to waive that company, to which he hath no love; nay, he doth in the whole course of his life prefer his swine, as the Gadarenes,[2] before his soul; set the servant on horseback and suffer the master to go on foot. His voice to religion is like the Jews' to the poor man in vile raiment, "Stand thou there, or sit thou here under my footstool;" and his words to the world are like theirs to the man in goodly apparel, "Come up hither, or sit thou here in a good place"....[3]

But every saint, like Solomon, first builds a house for God, and then for himself. Whoever be displeased, or whatever be neglected, he will take care that God be worshipped. Abraham's steward, when sent to provide a wife for Isaac, though meat were set before him, refused to eat till he had done his errand.[4] Godliness is the errand about which man is sent into the world; now, as faithful servants, we must prefer our message before our meat, and serve our master before ourselves.

---

2. Mark 5:1–17.

3. James 2:2–3.

4. Genesis 24:33.

16

Godliness must have Industry[1]

To make religion one's business, containeth to pursue it with industry in our conversations.[2] A man that makes his calling his business is not lazy, but laborious about it; what pains will he take! what strength will he spend! how will he toil and moil at it early and late! The tradesman, the husbandman, eat not the bread of idleness, when they make their callings their business; if they be good husbands, they are both provident to observe their seasons, and diligent to improve them for their advantage; they do often even dip their food in their sweat, and make it thereby the more sweet. Their industry appears in working hard in their callings, and in improving all opportunities for the furtherance of their callings.

1. Thus he that makes religion his business is industrious and laborious in the work of the Lord. The heart of his ground, the strength of his inward man, is spent about the good corn of religion, not about the weeds of earthly occasions. He makes haste to keep God's commandments[3]...and he is hot and lively in his devotion....[4] He believeth that to fear

---

1. Swinnock, *Christian Man's Calling*, 1:38–39, 41, 43.
2. I.e., life.
3. Leviticus 11:30.
4. Romans 12:11.

God with a secondary fear is atheism; that to trust God with a secondary trust is treason; that to honour God with a secondary honour is idolatry; and to love God with a secondary love is adultery; therefore he loveth (and he feareth and trusteth and honoureth) "the Lord his God, with all his heart, and with all his soul, and with all his strength"....[5] His measure of loving God is without measure....

2. The industry of a man about his calling, or whatsoever he makes his business, appeareth in his taking all advantages for the furtherance thereof. A tradesman that minds his employment, doth not only in his shop, but also abroad, and when he is from home, drive forward his trade...so the Christian that makes religion his business, is industrious to improve all opportunities for the furtherance of his general calling.... Whether the actions he be about be natural or civil, he makes them sacred; whether the company he be in be good or bad, he will mind his holy calling; whether he be riding or walking, whether it be at home or abroad; whether he be buying or selling, eating or drinking, whatsoever he be doing, or wheresoever he be going, still he hath an eye to further godliness, because he makes that his chief business....

---

5. Matthew 22:36–37.

17

Godliness must have Constancy[1]

To exercise ourselves to godliness, implieth to persevere in it with constancy to our dissolution.... They who make religion their business, are constant, immoveable, and do "always abound in the work of the Lord."[2] Their day of life is their labour; "the sun riseth, and man goeth to his labour until the evening."[3] Death only is their night of resting, when they die in the Lord; then, and not till then, they "rest from their labours"....

Water in the baths is always warm; as long as there is water, there is heat. Not so our ordinary water; though it may be warmed by the fire at present, yet if taken off it returns to its former coldness, nay, it is colder than before, because the spirits which kept it from the extremity of cold, are by the fire boiled out of it. The reason is plain; the heat of the baths is from an inward principle, and therefore is permanent; the heat of the latter is from an external cause, and therefore is inconstant.

That warmth of piety which proceeds from an inward principle of a purified conscience, is accompanied with perseverance; but that profession which

---

1. Swinnock, *Christian Man's Calling*, 1:44–45.
2. 1 Corinthians 15:58.
3. Psalm 104:23.

Nero (reign 54–68 AD)

floweth from an outward motive, where men, as chameleons, take their colour from that which stands next them, their religion from those they have their dependence upon, is of a short duration.

A man that minds religion by the by is like Nebuchadnezzar's image, he hath a head of gold, but feet of clay.[4] His beginning may be like Nero's[5] first five years, full of hope and encouragement, but afterwards, as a carcase, he is more filthy and unsavoury every day than other. His insincerity causeth his inconstancy. Trees unsound at the root, will quickly cease their putting forth of fruit. Such men, if godliness enjoy a summer of prosperity, may like a serpent creep on the ground, and stretch themselves at length, to receive the warmth of the sun, but if winter come he will creep into some ditch or dunghill, lest he should take cold....

He that only pretends towards religion, if a storm meet him in the way to heaven, he leaves it, and takes shelter in the earth; as a snail, he puts out his head to see what weather is abroad, (what countenance religion hath at court, whether great men do smile or frown upon the ways of God,) and if the heavens be lowering, he shrinks into his shell, esteeming that his only safety. But they that make godliness their business, do not steer their course by such cards—they follow their trade, though they meet with many trials; as resolved travellers, whether the ways be fair or foul, whether the weather be clear or cloudy, they

---

4. Daniel 2:31–33.

5. Nero was a Roman Emperor (54–68 AD). It is likely that both Paul and Peter were martyred at Rome during Nero's reign.

will go on towards their heavenly Canaan; "They go from strength to strength till they appear before God in Sion."[6]

---

6. Psalm 74:8.

SECTION FIVE

The Nature of Godliness

18

---- ❖ ----

What is Godliness?[1]

Godliness is a worshipping the true God in heart and life, according to his revealed will.[2] In this description of godliness, I shall observe four parts....

First, for the act, godliness is a worship. Worship comprehends all that respect which man oweth and giveth to his Maker. It is that service and honour, that fealty and homage, which the creature oweth and tendereth to the fountain of his being and happiness. It is the tribute which we pay to the King of kings, whereby we acknowledge his sovereignty over us, and our dependence on him. "Give unto the Lord the honour due unto his name; worship the Lord in the beauty of holiness."[3] To worship God is to give him the glory which is due him. It is a setting the crown of glory on God's head. To render him due honour is true holiness; to deny this, is atheism and irreligion. All that inward reverence and respect, and all that outward obedience and service to God, which the word enjoineth, is included in this one word worship....

Secondly, The object, the true God. All religion without the knowledge of the true God is a mere

---

1. Swinnock, *Christian Man's Calling*, 1:31–35.

2. Swinnock is expounding 1 Timothy 4:7 "But refuse profane and old wives' fables, and exercise thyself unto godliness."

3. Psalm 29:2.

notion, an airy, empty nothing. Divine worship is one of the chiefest jewels of God's crown, which he will by no means part with. God alone is the object of the godly man's worship....[4] God alone is to be worshiped, because he alone is worthy of worship. "Thou art worthy, O Lord, to receive glory, and honour, and power: for thou hast created all things."[5] To hold anything in opinion, or to have anything in affection for God, which is not God is idolatry....

Thirdly, The extent, in heart and life. Godliness is the worshipping God in the inward motions of the heart, and the outward actions of the life; where the spring of the affections is clear, and the stream of the conversation runs clear, there is true godliness.... Heart-godliness pleaseth God best, but life-godliness honours him most; the conjunction of both make a complete Christian. In a godly man's heart, though some sin be left, yet no sin is liked; in his life, though sin may remain, yet no sin reigns. His heart is suitable to God's nature, and his life is answerable to God's law, and thence he is fitly denominated a godly man....

Fourthly, The rule, according to his revealed will. Every part of divine worship must have a divine precept.... The institutions of Christ, not the inventions of men, are the rule of worship. Our work is not to make laws for ourselves or others, but to keep the laws which the great prophet of his church hath taught us; that coin of worship which is current amongst us must be stamped by God himself. We

---

4. Exodus 20:2.
5. Revelation 4:11.

are to be governed as the point in the compass, not by the various winds, (the practices of former ages, or the fashions of the present generation, which are mutable and uncertain,) but by the constant heavens. Our devotion must be regulated exactly according to the standard of the word. It is idolatry to worship a false god, or the true God in a false manner.

19

Godliness in Action[1]

As thy duty is to make religion thy business in religious, so also in natural actions A good scrivener is not only careful how he makes his first and great letters, his flourishes, but also the smallest letters, nay, his very stops and commas. A scribe instructed for the kingdom of heaven, is heedful not only that the weightiest actions of God's immediate worship, but also that the meaner[2] passages of his life, be conformable to God's law. A wise builder will make his kitchen as well as his parlour according to rule. A holy person turns his natural actions into spiritual, and whilst he is serving his body he is serving his God. It is said of a Scotch divine, that he did eat, drink, and sleep eternal life. Luther tells, that though he did not always pray and meditate, but did sometimes eat, and sometimes drink, and sometimes, sleep, yet all should further his account; the latter as truly, though not so abundantly as the former.[3] And indeed it is our privilege that natural actions may be adopted into the family of religion, and we may worship God as really at our tables as in his temple.

---

1. Swinnock, *Christian Man's Calling*, 1:260–261, 285, 287–288.

2. I.e., smaller.

3. Swinnock gives the reference as *Luther on Genesis 33.*

Saints must not, like brute beasts, content themselves with a natural use of the creatures, but use them as chariots to mount them nearer, and cords to bind them closer to God. Piety or holiness to the Lord must be written upon their pots.[4] "Whether ye eat or drink, or whatsoever ye do, do all to the glory of God"....[5]

My corrupt heart being prone to turn things lawful into fuel for lust, like the spider to suck poison out of the sweetest flowers, and to make what my God giveth me for a comfort, to prove, through the subtlety of the serpent, as Eve to Adam, a cross and a curse, I wish, in general, that whilst I use my meat, and drink, and sleep, and apparel, I may never abuse them, but that I may so ensure my right to them through Christ, the heir of all things, to taste the love of my God in them, and make such a holy and sanctified improvement of them, that I may have a spiritual title to natural good things; may hold all *in capite*,[6] and the things of this life may be whetstones to quicken my holiness, and loadstones to draw my affections nearer to heaven....

Finally, I wish that I may be so sensible of the worth of those narrow streams of time, because of their tendency to the boundless ocean of eternity, that, like holy Hooper,[7] I may be spare of sleep, sparer of diet, and sparest of time, that I may redeem

---

4. Zechariah 14:20.

5. 1 Corinthians 10:31.

6. i.e., in tenure; on loan.

7. John Hooper (d. 1555) was Bishop of Gloucester and Worcester. Because of his Protestant convictions, he was burned at the stake during the reign of Bloody Mary.

John Hooper (d. 1555)

it as much as may be convenient from those natural actions which are necessary; and that when eating, drinking, and clothing, and sleeping, and days, and weeks, and years, and ages shall be no more, I may eat of my Saviour's hidden manna, drink of the new wine in my Father's kingdom, be arrayed with the white linen of the saints, and inherit that rest which remaineth for the people of my God, for ever and ever. Amen.

20

─── ◦«(◦)»◦ ───

Godliness at Play[1]

Thy duty is to exercise thyself to godliness in thy recreations; the Christian in his walking, as well as in his
working, must be furthering his eternal weal. Our gar-
dens or places of delights, as well as our houses, must
be consecrated ground.... Reader, sacrifice thy recreations, thy joys, thy delights to God, and they shall all
live; it is rankness of them which God desireth should
be put to death. That these pleasures are not simply
unlawful, is plain, "Eat thy bread," saith God, "with
joy, drink thy wine with a merry heart; live joyfully
with the wife of thy youth."[2] Epicurism[3] is not at all
commanded, but moderate delight in creatures is
allowed and commended, "He gives all things richly
to enjoy"....[4] The merciful God is pleased, out of
his bounty, not only to allow his creatures what is

---

1. Swinnock, *Christian Man's Calling*, 1:288, 299–300.

2. Ecclesiastes 9:7–9.

3. Epicurism (or Epicureanism) is a philosophical system, established by Epicurus (342–270 BC). He believed that there are two
kinds of pleasure, stemming from two kinds of desire: natural and
vain. We must learn to satisfy our natural desires while denying our
vain desires. When we do, we experience pleasure (or happiness).
Epicurus' followers departed somewhat from his teaching. They
affirmed that people must satisfy all their desires. This is known as
hedonism.

4. 1 Timothy 6:17.

for necessity, but also what is for delight. Christian, it is more than God requireth of thee to be always pondering and poring on such subjects as make thy heart sad, whereby thou thyself art disadvantaged, banishing that cheerfulness from thee, which is an ornament to Christianity; and others discouraged, supposing that all who walk in heaven's way, must needs be, as thou art, mopish and melancholy. Piety doth regulate, but not extirpate our pleasures....

Recreations being the intermission of my labour, and spending of some time in delightful exercise, for the refreshing of my body and mind, which, by working much, are apt to tire and grow weary, I wish, in general, that I may never abuse this favour which my Master affordeth me (as some drunken servants) to make me unfit for his work, but may be so conscientious in observing those cautions about it, which his law prescribeth, that my vigour and strength being thereby repaired, I may after it follow his business with the more alacrity and ability....

Lord, let my chiefest and constant recreations be to walk with my beloved in the garden of thy word, to refresh my spiritual scent and sight with the fair and fragrant flowers of thy promises and precepts, to do the work which thou hast given me to do, and to enjoy fellowship with thyself in ordinances, till I come to that place where bodies are above such dreggy delights, and souls above all mediate communion, and thou thyself art all in all. Amen.

21

Godliness at Work[1]

As religion must be our business in our spiritual and
natural, so also in our civil actions and particular
callings. The heavenly bodies have an influence, not
only on men and women, but also on trees and plants.
The holiness of a saint must be operative, not only in
his more noble exercises, the ordinances of God, but
likewise in his earthly and inferior employments. Thy
duty is, reader, to mind thy general in thy particular
calling, and to drive a trade in heaven, whilst thou art
following thy trade on earth. When thou art called to
the Lord, thou art not called from thy labour; nay,
as thou art a servant of Christ, thou art bound to be
serviceable to thy country, in some mental or manual
calling; but thy diligence therein must proceed from
conscience, not from covetousness—from subjection
to God's word, not from affection to thy wealth.

As thy particular calling is the zodiac through
which thou daily passest, so godliness must be the
ecliptic line to go through the midst of it. Godliness
must be the key to open the shop; godliness must be
the whip to drive the cart; godliness must be the cock
to call thee up to thy work; godliness must be the
clock to call thee off from thy work; godliness must

---

1. Swinnock, *Christian Man's Calling*, 1:300–301, 304–305, 311,
313–314, 316, 319.

be the principle, the rule, and the end of thy work. *Holiness to the Lord* was written upon the bridles of the horses....[2]

First, Be diligent in thy calling.... Secondly, Deal righteously in thy calling.... Thirdly, Be careful that thy particular calling encroach not upon thy general.... Fourthly, If thou wouldst exercise thyself to godliness in thy particular calling, look up to God for a blessing upon thy labours therein.... Fifthly, If thou dost prosper in thy calling, let God alone have the praise.... Sixthly, Labour for contentedness, and a holy composedness in all conditions....

My particular calling being a peculiar and distinct station, wherein I am bound to be serviceable to my country and family, and wherein also I have this privilege, that I may further my general calling, if I mind it out of conscience to the Lord, and in obedience to his word, I wish, in general, that I may never cross the wise providence of my God, in the government of the world, by neglecting it, or thinking lightly of it; but since I am listed under the captain of my salvation, may serve him faithfully, not only in general as a soldier, but also in that place or office to which he hath chosen and called me....

In a word, I wish that I may, like the wise merchant, sell all I have to buy the pearl of great price; the gold tried in the fire, that I may be rich; the white raiment, that I may be clothed; and drive such a constant trade with my God in the other world, bearing from thence, and sending thither daily, that when the king of terrors shall give me a writ of ease from my

---

2. Zechariah 14:20.

particular calling, I may die in the Lord, rest from my labours, and have my works following me through free grace, into an exceeding and eternal weight of glory. Amen.

Aristotle (384–322 BC)

22

Godliness as a Parent[1]

It is thy duty to exercise thyself to godliness in thy family and relations. A Christian must not, like the Israelites' pillar in the wilderness, be light on one side and dark on the other, be diligent in one relation and negligent in another; but as a candle in a crystal lantern, be lightsome quite round it, be holy in every relation in which he standeth.

Reader, I shall consider thee as governor or governess of a family, and herein direct thee what thou shouldst do for the faithful discharge of thy trust in that relation....

A family is a natural and simple society of certain persons, having mutual relation one to another, under the private government of one head or chief. Aristotle[2] calleth families the first society in nature, and the ground of all the rest. Before the flood, the whole form of civil and ecclesiastical government was con-

---

1. Swinnock, *Christian Man's Calling*, 1:329–330, 334, 337–338, 342–349, 351–352.

2. Aristotle (384–322 BC) was a Greek philosopher. Swinnock displays an understanding of various philosophical systems but leans heavily upon Aristotle: the "prince." *Christian Man's Calling*, 1:425, 450, 478; 2:86, 203, 294; 3:407, 427; *Incomparableness of God*, 4:8. He employs aspects of Aristotle's thinking that serve his own purposes while avoiding any ultimate dependence upon this "blind heathen." *Christian Man's Calling*, 1:308; *Door of Salvation*, 5:37.

fined within the precincts of private families. A family is the epitome of a kingdom and a commonwealth in a little volume. The way to make godly parishes, and godly countries, and godly kingdoms, is to make godly families....

It concerneth thee, therefore, reader, nearly, to exalt godliness in thy house as well as in thy heart; nay, I will be bold to tell thee, if there be in thee the truth of religion, thou wilt propagate it amongst thy relations....

First, Be careful whom thou admittest into thy family. Art thou unmarried, and to choose a husband or wife? Do thy occasions call for a man-servant or maid-servant? Be careful where thou fixest; for, believe it, not only thy grace will appear in a good choice, but also godliness will be much hindered or furthered by thy choice. "One sinner destroyeth much good."[3] One man may pull down that house, which many, with much care, cost, and pains, did set up....

Secondly, Mind holy performances in thy family. Every master of a family is a priest, and his whole family should be a royal priesthood, offering at least morning and evening sacrifice to God, acceptable through Jesus Christ.... A foundation well laid by the master of a family is a great help to the minister when he goeth to rear and raise the building. Confident I am our work would not have half that difficulty which now it hath, if masters of families would but do their duties.... The ordinary duties in families are prayer, reading the word, with instructing children and servants out of it, and singing....

---

3. Ecclesiastes 9:18.

Thirdly, Set a good pattern to thy family. The fore-horse in the team had need to go right, because all the rest follow in the same road. If the commander be treacherous, how soon may he betray his soldiers, who follow him at the heels, into the enemy's hands! A governor of a family must, like Moses, be mighty both in word and deed. Patterns are very prevalent both to good and evil. Precepts teach, but examples draw.... If godliness be written in the book of thy life, in a fair character, in a large lovely letter, it may invite thy children and servants to read and like it, who otherwise possibly would not have taken the least notice of it....

Fourthly, Be careful and diligent that thy whole family may sanctify the Lord's day.... Do not suffer any of thine to be playing idly in the churchyard, when they should be praying earnestly in the church; nor to be talking vainly of the world, when they should be hearkening reverently to the word....

Fifthly, Let discipline be set up in thy family.... Thy duty is to "warn the unruly,"[4] to acquaint them of sin, how near and dear soever to thee, with the dishonour they bring thereby to God, the disgrace to the gospel, and the disadvantage and destruction to their own souls.... Let thy reproofs against sin be mingled with, and so managed that they may manifest, love to their souls. When the nail is dipped in grease it entereth without renting the board; when reprehension is dipped in, and tipped with love, it will probably enter the heart, without cutting it in pieces with rage and revenge....

---

4. 1 Thessalonians 5:13.

Sixthly, Take care that all in thy family be well employed; not to permit idleness in thy house is one way to prevent ungodliness. There is employment suitable to every person in thy dwelling; servants should be diligent in the discharge of their duties.... Children also, if at home, must be employed in their places; if young, in learning; if elder, in some calling....

Seventhly, Maintain peace and love in thy family. Contentions will hinder religion; strife, like fire, is wholly opposite to the water of grace.... Thy house should be a lesser heaven, in it thy God must be worshipped and glorified; but in heaven there are no storms; tempests ascend no higher than the middle region. Where God is served with perfect purity, there is perfect peace....

In a word, I wish that I may, like Cornelius,[5] fear the Lord with all my house; so govern it, according to God's law, that all in it may be under the influence of his love, and heirs of everlasting life. Lord, be thou pleased so to assist and prosper me in the management of this great and weighty trust, that my house may be thy house, my servants thy servants, my children thy children, and my wife belong to the spouse of thy dear Son, that so when death shall give a bill of divorce, and break up our family, we may change our place, but not our company; be all preferred from thy lower house of prayer to thine upper house of praise, where in neither marrying nor giving in marriage, but all are as angels, ever pleasing, worshipping, and enjoying thy blessed self...to whom be glory, hearty and universal obedience, for ever and ever. Amen.

---

5. Acts 10:1–2.

23

Godliness as a Child[1]

It is the glory and credit of children to drink in the dews of godliness in the morning of their lives. Oh, it is a lovely sight to behold those trees blossoming with the fruits of the Spirit in the spring of their age; to behold one that is fourteen for the greenness of his age, to be forty in the graciousness of his carriage....

I proceed to the duties of children to parents.

The first duty is reverence. There is a distance between children and parents; therefore there must be reverence from children to parents. "A son honoureth his father."[2] The difference in age commands honour.... This reverence must be inward in heart. Children should have awful apprehensions of their parents as their superiors, as those to whom they are engaged, under God, both for their beings and breedings....[3] This reverence must be outward in life, and that both in language and carriage....

Secondly, Obedience.... "Children, obey your parents in the Lord, for this is right."[4] In which sentence the apostle delivereth both the reason and the

---

1. Swinnock, *Christian Man's Calling*, 1:438, 447–448, 450, 453–455, 458, 463–464.

2. Malachi 1:6.

3. Leviticus 19:3.

4. Ephesians 6:1.

rule of children's obedience. The reason is, "for this is right;" it is agreeable to righteousness that thou shouldst yield subjection to them, to whom thou hast so many and such great obligations. It is right by the law of God, of nature, and of nations. The rule is "in the Lord," that is, in lawful, not in sinful commands....

Thirdly, Submission. Children must not only be subject to their father's precepts, but also submit to their punishments. "We have had fathers of the flesh which corrected us, and we gave them reverence"....[5] Reader, if thy parents reprove or chastise thee, it is for thy profit; and wilt thou grumble at that which tendeth to thy good? Alas! they punish thee here, that thou mayest not perish for ever. Besides, they correct thee because God commands them; and canst thou be displeased at them because they dare not displease God?....

Fourthly, Affection. Children are bound to love their parents, and their obedience must grow upon this root. He is not a son, but a slave, that serveth his father merely out of fear; filial and servile obedience are opposite. As parents are tender of their children, so children ought to be tender of their parents....

Fifthly, Gratitude. It is thy duty to requite their care and cost upon thee; thy body, and time, and estate, should not be thought too much for them; the law of God, as well as the law of man, doth command children to relieve their necessitous parents to their power. "But if any widow have children or nephews, let them first learn to shew piety at home,

---

5. Hebrews 12:9.

and to requite their parents, for this is good and acceptable before God."[6] It is observable, children's kindness to their parents is termed ευσεβεια, piety or godliness, because it is a part thereof and very acceptable to God....

The relation of a child, speaking my great and manifold obligations to my parents, under God, for my conception, birth, and breeding, besides those many cares and fears which are incident for my sake to their tender yearning bowels; for which I am engaged by the law of God, of nature, and of nations, to be grateful and dutiful; I wish in general that I may never be so far possessed of the devil, like him in the Gospel whom no cords could hold,[7] as to break all these bonds in sunder, but may behave myself towards my parents on earth as an obedient child of my Father in heaven. Lord, whilst others pretend much religion abroad, but manifest little piety at home, make me so conscientious of all thy commands that I may not be unmindful of my debts to others, but be sure to pay my duty, my specialties, to them....

In a word, I wish that I may so imitate their gracious patterns, so submit to their wholesome rebukes, so obey their pious precepts, yield them such hearty reverence, and in all things demean myself so dutifully, that God may be my father, and own me for his son or daughter; that my God may spare me as a man spareth his son that serveth him; that I may have a name within the house of my God better than of sons and daughters; and that when all these rela-

---

6. 1 Timothy 5:4.
7. Mark 5:1–17.

tions…shall cease, my days may be long in the land of promise which the Lord my God hath given me for possession, and I may enjoy the glorious liberty and endless blessed life of the sons of God amongst the congregation of the first-born. Amen.

24

Godliness as a Spouse[1]

Marriage is the lawful conjunction of one man and one woman for the term of their natural lives, for the generation of children, the avoiding of sin, or the comfort of mutual society.... Reader, if God hath called thee to this relation, walk worthy of it, behave thyself in it, as one married to Christ. God did not institute marriage to be a hindrance, but to be a help to religion....

1. For arguments to conscientiousness in this state, (1) Consider the dignity of marriage. Marriage is honourable, and therefore thy carriage in it must be answerable. An honourable relation calls for a holy conversation.... (2) Consider the frailty of the married.... The season of married persons' abode together is short.... Wise persons, when they are called to places which they must enjoy for a short time, will make the most of them....

2. I shall now speak to the duties incumbent on this relation....

First, Amity. This is the nearest relation, and therefore requireth the dearest affection. They are one in many bonds: they have one name, and therefore should have one nature; they are one in the fruit of

---

1. Swinnock, *Christian Man's Calling*, 1:464–468, 471–472, 475, 477, 481–482.

their loins, and hence should be one in love.[2] They are one body, one flesh, and so should have but one soul, one spirit; they have one bed, one board, one house, and therefore should be one in heart. The love betwixt Christ and his spouse, which is so fervent that she is sick of love to him, and he died for love to her,[3] is set out by the love betwixt husband and wife, to shew how great this love is, or at least ought to be. Without the union of hearts, the union of bodies will be no benefit. Where the obligation is greatest, there the affection must be strongest. The husband ought to love his wife, and she him, above father, mother, children, and all others in the world....

Second, Fidelity. Husbands and wives must be faithful to each other. They are partners in the nearest degree imaginable; and therefore, if unfaithful, the most foolish thieves that are possible. This faithfulness must shew itself in reference to their estates, names, and bodies.... Men must have the highest thoughts of their own wives, and women of their own husbands, and then they will not look so as to lust after others....

Marriage being a condition which requireth much circumspection as it is a relation of the sweetest and nearest communion in this world, ordained by our God, both for the increase of his church, and our mutual comfort, and as it is the first relation in nature, and the original of all the rest, upon the wrong management of which the ruin of the other doth frequently follow; we wish in general that our behaviour

---

2. Job 19:17.

3. Song of Solomon 2:4; John 15:13.

in it may never be so void of conscience as to turn it into a cross to ourselves or a curse to others, but that our fellowship together may be such that we may both in it have fellowship with the Father, and with Jesus Christ his Son.

Lord, who art the guide of all relations, and the God of all grace, be pleased to grant us affections suitable to our condition, that our whole carriage therein may be as becometh Christians, and such as are married to the Lord Christ; that as Abraham and Sarah, we may be famous for faith; as Isaac and Rebecca, we may live together in the dearest love; and that, as that pious pair, Zacharias and Elizabeth, we may walk in all the commandments and statutes of the Lord blameless, and we, walking in company, may walk the more cheerfully in the way which leadeth to everlasting life.

25

Godliness in Prosperity[1]

Prosperity is a condition which consisteth in the fruition of outward good things, as health, strength, friends, riches, honours, and the like. As a constellation is a collection of many stars, so a prosperous condition is a confluence of many temporal comforts. God in his wise providence is pleased to give some persons large draughts of these sugared pleasures, their cup runneth over. They are in themselves mercies for which we may pray with humble submission, and for which we must praise God with holy affections; but through the corruption of our hearts, they often prove prejudicial to holiness. Those fires which were made to warm us, do often black and burn us. Small vessels carrying a great sail are apt to be overturned with every tempest....

My work now is to persuade thee in the tide of prosperity to be profitable to thy own soul, and serviceable to the blessed God.... I shall...lay down some directions for thy carriage in prosperity, and shew thee wherein the power of godliness, or the making religion thy business in that condition, consisteth.

---

1. Swinnock, *Christian Man's Calling*, 2:47–49, 53, 55–56, 59, 61, 63–69, 74.

First, Be especially watchful against those sins which a prosperous estate is most liable to. As there are sins proper to every calling, and to every constitution, so also to every condition.... In general, take heed of atheism; let not earthly prosperity lessen either thy love to, or labour for, heavenly things. When there is much wool on a sheep's back, it is sometimes caught in the thorns and famished. Much wealth, much bodily mercy, hath many times so hampered and entangled a man, that his soul is starved.... In particular, take heed of pride, carnal confidence, and senselessness of others' sufferings, which three sins prosperous men are prone to....

Second, Value thyself, not by thy estate in this, but by thy inheritance in the other, world. Grace will teach a saint in poverty to have all things, and yet to possess nothing.[2] It is a sure sign of saintship when a Christian, in the greatest confluence of creatures, can rate himself only by his estate in the covenant; and a special part of godliness for a person who hath large possessions to overlook all, and esteem himself wholly by his eternal portion.... Rate thyself by thy treasure in heaven, by the pardon of thy sins, by thine interest in Christ, and by the durable riches and righteousness. These only are the mercies which are worth thousand millions; others are but painted cards and brass counters to these. Outward mercies serve the flesh, and last for a brittle life; but these mercies concern the soul and relate to eternity.

Third, Let God alone have the glory of outward mercies; do not crown thine own head with laurel,

---

2. 1 Corinthians 7:31.

but pay thy rent of laud and praise to God alone, who is the true landlord.... It is God's bounty which filleth thy heaps, and therefore his glory must fill thy heart. Art thou rich? "The Lord maketh poor, and maketh rich."[3] He maketh their persons; the needy and wealthy are both his workmanship....

Fourth, Love God the more for the mercies he bestoweth on thee. We ought indeed to love God principally for himself. His own perfections, not our possessions, must be the original of our affection. That servant is mercenary who worketh only for wages; and that love of a wife is spurious which is placed on the husband's portion. True love is fixed on his person; yet as fire which hath fuel enough to burn of itself, flameth out the more by having oil poured upon it, so the mercies which flow from God must increase that fire of a Christian's love, which is founded in, and abundantly fed by, those excellences that are in God....

Fifth, Do God the more abundant service. The more liberally God soweth, the more liberally he should reap. The more wages men give, the more work they expect. Where the sun shineth hottest, there are the biggest and best fruits.... "Charge them that are rich in this world, that they do good, and be rich in good works."[4] Those that are rich in goods and wealth, must be rich in good works. To do a little good will not be sufficient for them who have received much good....

---

3. 1 Samuel 2:7.

4. 1 Timothy 6:17–18.

Sixth, In prosperity, prepare for adversity. Summer will not last all year, therefore men provide for winter. The wind will not always set in one corner. The south wind of prosperity now bloweth, but expect the north wind of adversity.... Reader, now God giveth thee health and strength, and Sabbaths and seasons of grace, do not loiter, but improve them to the uttermost, in laying up a good foundation against the time of need. Alas! thou knowest not how soon the weather may alter. God may speedily call thee to great changes in thy life....

A prosperous condition, being a sweet fruit of divine beneficence, and a strong obligation to obedience, both as it encourageth me to serve so bountiful a master, and as it affordeth me more talents and instruments of doing his work, I wish that I may never turn his grace into wantonness, nor suffer the showers of heaven's mercy to increase or ripen the weeds of my corruptions; but that as the heat of the sun putteth out the fire, so the warm beams of divine love may extinguish the fire of lust in my soul, and my heart may be so affected with his bounty as to be the more abundant in duty.

26

——— ◆ ———

Godliness in Adversity[1]

Adversity is a condition of life which consisteth in the want of outward good things, and presence of outward evil things, as sickness, disgrace, poverty, imprisonment, and the like.... My work, reader, is to direct thee how thou mayest, like Samson, fetch meat out of this eater,[2] and take this physic which is so unpleasing to thy flesh, for the greatest profit and advantage of thy spirit....

As to the nature of making religion thy business in this condition, it consisteth partly in avoiding those sins which an afflicted estate is prone to, as despising God's hand, impatience, envying at those who prosper; and partly in exercising those graces which are required, and proper in adversity, as faith, rejoicing in the Lord, contentedness with thy condition, &c. But I shall propound them to thee in these particulars.

First, Be sensible of God's hand; it is a sin to faint under it, but it is a duty to feel it: "My son, despise not thou the chastening of the Lord, nor faint when thou art rebuked of him."[3] A Christian must carefully avoid these two extremes of despising the chastening

---

1. Swinnock, *Christian Man's Calling*, 2:82, 84, 92–94, 97–98, 101, 103, 107, 111–114, 161.

2. Judges 14:8–9.

3. Hebrews 12:5.

of the Lord, or despairing when he is chastened, and walk in the golden mean between them both....

[Secondly,] As thy duty is to be sensible of God's hand, so also to be submissive to it. Though we must groan and feel God's hand, yet we must not grumble and fret at his dealings. Obedience is due to his severest precepts, and patience is thy duty under the sharpest providence. He is too just to be questioned, too good to be suspected, and too great to be quarrelled with....

Thirdly, Justify God in the greatest affliction which befalleth thee. Doth God lay heavy things on thee, in the loss of thy health, or estate, or liberty? Have thou high thoughts of him.... In the darkest night of dread and terror, saints can see the righteousness of God to sparkle gloriously.... The pain which we feel is of our own procuring; the rods which scourge us are of our own gathering; our own wickedness is the original of our woe; the web in which we are entangled, like the spider's, is woven out of our own bowels; we obeyed not his voice....

Fourthly, Wait God's leisure for deliverance. There is a twofold patience required in every Christian. (1) A patience of bearing the evil inflicted; and, (2) A patience of forbearing the good promised. God, indeed, hath engaged to deliver his people out of all their troubles; but between the seed-time of the promise, and the harvest of the performance, a sharp winter often interposeth; therefore the Christian must wait....

Fifthly, Rejoice in God in the meantime. Saints are compared to lilies, afflictions to thorns. The lily is fresh, and looks fair in the midst of thorns. A Christian may be cheerful under the heaviest bodily cross. He hath fair weather overhead, the sunshine of God's favour, therefore he may go merrily on though it be dirty under feet....

Sixthly, Take heed of envying wicked men in prosperity. Men who are at the bottom of the hill, are apt to envy those that are at the top. When David was chastened every morning, and in great adversity: "I was envious at the foolish," saith he, "when I saw the prosperity of the wicked."[4] "When I saw;" his sight was an inlet to this sin.... Those especially who are afflicted, are prone to conceive evil at the good which others receive. He who doth but consider the state of the wicked, will rather pity than envy them in the most prosperous condition....

Lastly, Study and answer God's end in thy afflictions. This indeed, though named last, is the first and chiefest of all. The errand upon which a messenger is sent from a great prince is much to be minded. It is not enough to forbear fretting at him, or to rejoice with him, but to interpret his language, to spell out his meaning, is required.... God's ends in afflicting are divers. First, It may be to try and discover thee to thyself; to try the strength of grace.... Secondly, It may be to purge out some sin which thou harbourest; the stock is purged by salt water.... Thirdly, It may be, the end of God in afflicting thee is to increase thy graces....

Lord, help me, whilst I am here in these lower regions, amidst such boisterous winds and waters, to endure all with patience, to be a gainer by every

---

4. Psalm 73:3.

providence, and in all things so to obey thy precepts, that when my body shall be parted from my soul, my soul may be parted from all these sufferings, and translated to thine upper region of heaven, whither those vapours which cause these storms and tempests can never ascend; where all tears shall be wiped from my eyes; where thou wilt give me beauty for ashes, the garment of gladness for the spirit of heaviness, (and, after all my grievous conflicts with the flesh, the world, and the wicked one,) a crown of glory on my head, a song of triumph in my mouth, a palm of victory in my hand, and to reign with Christ for ever and ever. Amen.

27

---•-‹(•)›-‹---

Godliness in Company[1]

God never intended that the world should be a wilderness, nor the chief inhabitants thereof, as barbarous beasts, to live alone, lurking in their dens. Monks, and nuns, and hermits, who, under pretence of sanctity, sequester themselves from all society, are so far from more holiness, and being better Christians, than others, that they seem to have put off the very human nature, and not to be so much as men....

Company is both comfortable and profitable. The pelican avoideth other birds, and keeps alone, but her tone is always sorrowful. Christians walk more merrily in the way of God's commandments, when they have many fellow-travellers....

I come now to shew wherein the power of godliness consisteth, or how a man maketh religion his business in the choice of his companions.

First, Be as careful as thou canst, that the persons thou choosest for thy companions be such as fear God.... Thou art far from walking after the good Spirit, if thou choosest to converse with open sepulchres, and such as are dead in sins and trespasses....

Secondly, If thou wouldst manifest godliness in the choice of thy companions, thy care must be, not

---

1. Swinnock, *Christian Man's Calling*, 2:238–239, 254, 257–258, 261, 267, 269.

St. Anthony (ca. 251–356), the so-called father
of monasticism, who isolated himself in Egypt's
Nitrian Desert (Wadi El Natrun today).

only to choose such as are godly, but also to choose them because they are godly. As godliness must be a ruling quality in them that are chosen, so it must be the ground of thy choice…. When God's grace in them is the only ground of our choice, and God's image on them the chief loadstone of our love, then we exercise ourselves to godliness in the choice of our companions….

Thirdly, In thy choice, have respect to spiritual ends, and accordingly improve it. Attend and intend thy own and thy companions' soul good in it. Friendship hath a key to the heart which it may use, not only to let itself into its secrets, but also to introduce its own conceptions. He hath a great advantage of persuading another to, and encouraging him, in holiness, who is already entertained as his friend into his heart. Where the person is so acceptable, the instruction will be the more welcome….

The blessed and glorious God, the Father of mercies, and foundation of all communion, of whom the whole family in heaven and earth is named, who hath sufficiently evidences the good of companions in saying, It is not good for man to be alone,[2] and who hath sanctified society by his own example in creating angels and men, not only for mutual comfort in the fruition of each other, but also that his sacred Majesty, and those heaven-born spirits, might have fellowship together, as intimate friends, and especially in that infinite complacency which he had in his beloved Son, and his Son in him from all eternity, who was daily his delight, rejoicing always before

---

2. Genesis 2:18.

him; having made me rational, and thereby meet for converse with men, religious, and thereby capable of communion with Christians, I wish that I may never abuse his kindness by shutting up myself, as monks and nuns, in cells or cloisters, or as some melancholy persons, in a closet or chamber; but may know both how to be alone, and how to be in company, and be so sensible of his love in affording me fellow-travellers, that my journey to my Father's house may be the more pleasant, that I may accept it thankfully, and improve it faithfully to his own praise....

Oh, cause thy servant so to glorify thee in my choice of companions, and in my carriage in all companies, that I may come at last to enjoy immediate communion with thy beautiful saints and thy blessed Majesty, world without end. Amen.

28

Godliness in Solitude[1]

A gracious person is not only conscientious in company, but also when he is alone; his whole life is nothing else but a walking with his God. "When I awake I am still with thee."[2] He no sooner opened the eyes of his body in the morning, but he was lifting up the eyes of his mind to heaven; when he was alone in his bed, he was in company with his God. As God was still with him, so he was still with God.... A saint, therefore, sequestereth himself from the noise and clamour of company, and worldly business, that he might have the more free and intimate converse with his Redeemer....

First, If thou wouldst exercise thyself to godliness when thou art alone, guard thy heart against vain thoughts; this is the first work to be done, without which all that I have to commend to thee will be in vain. It is to no purpose to expect that a glass should be filled with costly wine, when it is filled already with puddle water.... Some persons, though poor, when they are solitary, delight in the fancies and imaginations of great preferments, and pleasures, and riches, as if they were real, whereas they are the mere

---

1. Swinnock, *Christian Man's Calling*, 2:403–404, 412–415, 417, 424–425, 450–453.

2. Psalm 139:18.

chimeras and fictions of their own brains, and have no existence, but in their thoughts.... Others please themselves in the thoughts of sinful sports, or cheats, or unclean acts, and sit brooding on such cockatrice' eggs with great delight; it is their meat and drink to roll those sugarplums under their tongues. Though they cannot act sin outwardly for want of strength of body, or of a fit opportunity, yet they act sin inwardly with great love and complacency....[3] Others entertain themselves with needless and useless thoughts, such as tend neither to the informing the mind, nor reforming the heart or life. Like vagrants, a man meets with these in every place, but can neither tell whence they come, nor wither they go; they have neither a good cause not do they produce any good effect.... Christian be careful when thou art out of company, as well as in it, for these guests will visit thee as soon as ever thou art alone; and if thou shouldst not frown upon them, they will turn thy solitude into a crowd....

Secondly, If thou wouldst exercise thyself to godliness in solitude, labour to spiritualise earthly things. I must say this is one of the most excellent and enriching arts in Christianity.... He that hath learned this mystery is the true chemist; he leaves the dregs and lees of things, and extracts the substance and quintessence of them.... God hath given us three books, which we ought to be studying whilst we are living: the book of conscience, the book of Scripture, and the book of the creature; in the book of conscience we may read ourselves, in the book of the creature we may read God, in the book of Scripture we may read

---

3. I.e., satisfaction.

both God and ourselves. The great God sets us excellent lectures in the volume of the creation; though this book hath but three leaves in it, heaven, earth, seas, yet it teacheth us many rare lessons.... Reader, it is thy privilege that thou mayest perform this duty in any place....

Thirdly, If thou wouldst exercise thyself to godliness in solitude, mind solemn and set meditation.... Occasional meditations are like loving strangers, that afford us a visit, but are quickly gone. Deliberate meditations are as inhabitants that dwell with us, and are longer helpful to us.... Solemn meditation is a serious applying the mind to some sacred subject, till the affections be warmed and quickened, and the resolution heightened and strengthened thereby, against what is evil, and for that which is good....

Fourthly, If thou wouldst exercise thyself to godliness in solitude, accustom thyself to soliloquies, I mean to conference with thyself. He needs never be idle that hath so much business to do with his own soul.... Commune with your own hearts; when ye have none to speak with, talk to yourselves. Ask yourselves for what end ye were made, what lives ye have led, what times ye have lost, what love ye have abused, what wrath ye have deserved.... Self-communion will much help to curb your headstrong, ungodly passions. Serious consideration, like the casting up of earth among bees, will allay inordinate affections when they are full of fury, and make such a hideous noise....

Fifthly, In solitude, accustom thyself to secret ejaculations and converses with God. Lovers cast many a glance at each other, when they are at a distance, and are deprived of set meetings. A little boat may do us some considerable service, when we have not time to make ready a great vessel. The casting of our eyes and hearts up to heaven, will bring heaven down to us: "My meditations of him shall be sweet."[4]

---

4. Psalm 104:34.

29

Godliness on a Week Day[1]

Every day with a godly man is a holy Sabbath to the Lord. Godliness is not his holy day's, or high day's, but every day's work, and his exercise every part of every day: "I have inclined my heart to keep thy statutes," not by fits and starts, but "always unto the end."[2] The flower called heliotropium or turn-sol, turneth its face towards the sun from morning to night, so doth the true Christian towards the Sun of righteousness. The command of the Lord is: "Be thou in the fear of the Lord all the day long"....[3]

Reader, this present day's work may be the last act of thy life, it behoveth thee therefore to do it well. When thou art in thy closet, thou mayest think with thyself, I may possibly never pray more, never read the word of God more; how reverently, uprightly, graciously, should I therefore pray and read! When thou art eating or drinking, or refreshing nature, thou mayest consider, for aught I know, this may be the last time that I may use these creatures of God; how fearful should I be of abusing them! How should I eat my bread as before the Lord! When thou art in

---

1. Swinnock, *Christian Man's Calling*, 2:485, 488, 490, 499–501, 503, 505–508, 510–511.

2. Psalm 119:112.

3. Proverbs 23:17.

thy shop, or about thy calling, thou mayest ponder this, Possibly my last sand is running, and I must this day bid adieu for ever to wares and shops, and flocks and fields, and all civil commerce; oh, how heavenly should I be about these earthly affairs! How spiritual about these temporal things! Who would not do his last work well! Ah, how holy should he be at all times, who hath cause every moment to expect the coming of a holy and jealous God, to call him to an account....

As to the exercising thyself to godliness on a week-day...I shall commend to the reader six particulars.

First, Begin the day with God. Never expect a good day unless you begin with a good duty. He hath the best good-morrow who meets God first in the morning. Though some sunshiny mornings are overcast before night, yet the heavens are usually all day clear to him that sets out early in the way of its first serious exercise in the morning. When the right watch or clock is wound up well in the morning, it will be regularly going and moving all day after. He that loseth his heart in the morning in a throng of worldly affairs seldom finds it to purpose in any part of the day....

Secondly, Spend the greatest part of the day in thy particular calling. He that mindeth not his closet before his shop is an atheist; and he that mindeth not his shop after his closet is a hypocrite. The world is God's great family, and he will allow none in it to be idle.... It is a worthy speech of Master Bolton's, He is a cursed drone, a child of idleness, the very tennis-ball of temptation, most unworthy the blessings and benefits of human society, who doth not one way or

Robert Bolton (1572–1631)

other co-operate and contribute to the common good, with his best endeavours, in some honest particular calling....[4]

Thirdly, Be watchful all the day long. If thou wouldst walk safely, walk as one that hath eyes in his head. Ponder the paths of thy feet.... There is no Christian but walks as dangerously as he that danceth on the ropes; it behoves him therefore to walk watchfully. The children of God are called to be soldiers, to fight a good fight of faith,[5] under Christ, the captain of their salvation; but soldiers must be on their guard, especially such as are encompassed on all sides, at all times, with enemies of all sorts.... Watch especially against thy own sin. This is, as the Philistines said of David,[6] the great destroyer of the country, the great destroyer of thy conscience....

Fourth, Be careful to redeem time. Look upon thy time as one of the most precious talents which thy God hath intrusted thee with, and which he will reckon with thee for, and therefore not to be vainly spent, or needlessly squandered away. They are worthy to be punished, that spend their gold and silver lavishly, and waste their estates prodigally; but of how much sorer punishment are they worthy of that are prodigal and lavish of time, that is far more precious than gold and silver!.... A good man that liveth all the day long in the fear of his God, and husbands

4. Robert Bolton (1572–1631) was a Puritan divine. As given by Swinnock, the reference is *Directions for Walking with God, 49*. It was first published in 1625 as *Some generall Directions for a comfortable Walking with God*.

5. 1 Timothy 6:12.

6. 1 Samuel 29:1–6.

his time to the best advantage of his soul, finds it so sufficient for his work, that he is always ready to be called to an account and whenever he dieth, he dieth full of days, and hath had his full of living....

Fifth, Call thyself to an account at evening. Take a review of thy carriage the whole day, how thou didst behave thyself.... Put every night some brief queries to thy conscience upon these few heads: How did I behave myself in religious duties, in natural actions, in my particular calling, in recreations, if any were used, in company, and in solitude? Compare the carriage of thy heart and life herein, to the word and law of God; bring all to the touchstone....

Sixth, Close the day with God, in praying, and reading his word, both in thy closet and family. Our bed is resembled to our graves, sleep to death; it is of worse consequence to go to bed before we have made our prayers, than to our graves before we have made our wills. God is the first and the last, and ought to be the beginning and ending of every day....

The rock of ages, and everlasting Father, to whom a thousand years are but as one day, having out of his rich mercy afforded me a short time in this world, not to play or toy with temporal things, but to prepare my soul for my blessed eternity, I wish that I may never waste that precious season, which is given me for the working out of my own salvation, about needless affairs, but mind the one thing necessary, and pass the whole time of my sojourning here in the fear of my God....

30

Godliness in Death[1]

Thy duty is to exercise thyself to godliness, if God give thee opportunity, on a dying bed. The work of a saint is to glorify God, not only in his life, but also in his death. The silk-worm stretcheth out herself before she spin, and ends her life in her long-wrought clew. The Christian must stretch out himself on his dying bed, and end his life in the work of his Lord. Every man by his death payeth his debt to nature. He is earth in regard of his original creation, and must be earth in regard of his ultimate resolution: "Dust thou art, and to dust thou shalt return."[2] The sinner, when he dieth, payeth his debt to sin, Satan, and the law. To sin, as he is the servant of unrighteousness, and so must receive its wages, which is death; to Satan, as he hath sold himself to work wickedness at his will, and so must have his tempter to be his eternal tormentor; to the law, as he hath violated is precepts and commands, and therefore must undergo its punishment and curse. The saint, when he dieth, payeth his debt to God, for he oweth him honour as well by his death as by his life....

---

1. Swinnock, *Christian Man's Calling*, 3:38, 40, 48, 51–53, 55, 57–60, 69, 88–89.

2. Genesis 3:19.

The blessed Prince, and Lord of life, should be our pattern at death. He got his Father most glory, he did his church most good, by his death, though he was eminently serviceable to both all his lifetime....

I come now to shew wherein thou oughtest to exercise thyself to godliness, on a dying bed.

First, In commending God and his ways to others. The words of dying men are living oracles, and do not die with them. It is the unhappiness of worldlings and wicked men, that when they come to die, they cannot commend the work that they have followed, the wages which they have merited, or the master whom they have served; but it is the privilege of Christians, that they have cause to praise the sweetness of that love which they have tasted, the equity of those laws which they have obeyed, the grace, and mercy, and bounty, and faithfulness of that Lord whom they have prayed to, and delighted in, and worshipped, and the vastness, and richness, and certainty, and eternity of that reward which they are going to possess....

Secondly, In commending thyself and others to God by prayer. When the body breathes shortest, it breathes quickest. Though the Christian on is death-bed may want strength for long solemn devotion, his short ejaculations[3] should be both fervent and frequent.... (1) The sick man should pray especially for himself. Lord Jesus receive my spirit, saith Stephen;[4] Father, into thy hands I commend my spirit, saith Christ;[5]

---

3. I.e., spontaneous petitions.

4. Acts 7:59.

5. Luke 23:46.

Theodore Beza (1519–1605)

Lord, saith dying Beza,[6] perfect that which thou hast begun, that I suffer not shipwreck in the haven.... (2) For his relations. The more hot our affection is to any, the more fervent our petitions should be for them.... (3) For the whole church of God.... When we are dying, and going to the church triumphant, we should be sure to put up some requests for the poor members of Christ, and the church militant. Calvin was heard before his death often to sigh out, How long, Lord, how long will it be ere thou avenge the blood of thy servants?.... (4) For his benefactors, and those that have done good to him and his.... (5) For our enemies. This is to follow God's pattern, who doth good for evil, and to obey his precept, who commandeth us to pray for them that despitefully use us....[7]

Thirdly, In a holy exercise of faith, courage, repentance, charity, and patience. (1) Faith. It is the character of God's children that they live by faith, and they die in the faith....[8] (2) Courage. A Christian should be a volunteer in death. Many of the martyrs were as willing to die as to dine; went to the fire as cheerfully as to a feast, and courted its pale and ghastly countenance as if it had been a beautiful bride.... (3) Repentance.... Oh, how should the soul of a dying saint be inflamed with anger against sin, when he considers the rich love that it abuseth, the glorious name that it dishonoureth, the blessed Sav-

---

6. Theodore Beza (1519–1605) became the leader of the Swiss Calvinists after the death of Calvin.

7. Luke 23:34; Acts 7:60.

8. Habakkuk 2:6; Hebrews 11:31.

iour that it pierceth, and that vast happiness which he is going to possess, of which, without infinite grace and mercy, it had deprived him.... (4) Charity in a double respect. In forgiving them that have wronged thee.... In remembering the poor and afflicted, if God hath made thee able.... (5) Patience and submission to the will of God, both as to our death or life, and also as to our pain or ease in sickness.... He is the most valiant person that can die willingly when God would have him die, and live as willingly when God would have him live....

The righteous God having appointed death to be the end of all the children of men, as the common road through which they pass into the other world, to receive according to what they have done in this life, whether it be good, or whether it be evil, I wish that I may be wise to consider of my latter end, and so live that I may rather desire than be afraid to die; that my last days may be my best days, and I may imitate my Redeemer in bringing my God much honour, and doing his church much service, when I am entering my Master's joy....

Oh, when the sun of my life shall be setting, let the Sun of righteousness so arise upon me, that I may be delivered from the power, curse, and sting of death, and may find it, through his merits, to be my haven of rest, after all my foul weather; a bed of ease, after my sore labour; a release out of prison, and my jubilee to give me possession of an inheritance undefiled, incorruptible, that fadeth not away, which is reserved in heaven for me. Amen.

SECTION SIX

The Means
to Godliness

31

Lay a Good Foundation in a Renewed Heart and Nature[1]

If thou wouldst exercise thyself to godliness, be sure that thou layest a good foundation in a renewed heart and nature. I begin with this, because it is the chiefest requisite, and the basis of all. Godliness must first spring up in the heart, before it can overflow in the life. Other means are like those parts of the body, the want of which may be supplied by others; but this is like the heart, if wanting, nothing can make up its want. A dead man will as soon arise and walk, as an unsanctified person make religion[2] his business....

The heart of man is like the spring of the clock, which causeth the wheels to move, right or wrong, well or ill. Hence it is that God's precept is to this, "Make you a new heart, and a new spirit;"[3] and his promise of this, "I will put my fear into their hearts, and they shall never depart away from me."[4] The fear of God in the heart will bind thee fast to God in thy life. If the heart be thoroughly drawn to him, the tongue and hand will not depart from him. If the heart once set forward for God, all the members will follow

---

1. Swinnock, *Christian Man's Calling*, 3:89–90, 92.

2. I.e., true religion

3. Ezekiel 18:31.

4. Jeremiah 32:40.

after: the mouth will praise, the ears will attend to him, the eye will watch him, the feet will go after him; all the parts, like dutiful handmaids, in their places, will wait on their mistress. There was a great master among the Jews, which bid his scholars to consider and tell him, What was the best thing, or the best way, in which a man should always keep? One said, A good companion was the best thing in the world. Another said, A good neighbour was the best thing he could wish. A third said, A wise man, or one that could foresee future things. A fourth said, A good eye, that is, a liberal disposition. At last came one Eleazar, and he said, A good heart is better than them all. True, said the master, thou hast comprehended in two words all that the rest have said; for a good heart will make a man both contented, and a good companion, and a good neighbour, and help him to foresee things that are to come, that he may know what is on his part to be done. Indeed, without this there can be no godliness; all professions and performances are but a show, a shadow; and where there is this, there is all godliness in all manner of conversation. As the king of France said of Dover, that it was the key to England, and if his son, who then invaded the Britons, had not that, he had nothing; so it may be said of the heart, it is the key of the whole man,—it opens and shuts the door to godliness and wickedness,—and if grace hath not this, it hath nothing....

Till trees are grafted, and their nature altered, all the fruit they bring forth is wild and harsh, and little worth; till the Christian is grafted into Christ, and a new and another nature be infused into him, all his fruit is unsavoury and unacceptable to God, vain and unprofitable to himself....

32

⊱ ⋆《◦》⋆ ⊰

Live by Faith[1]

If thou wouldst exercise thyself to godliness, live by faith. The life of faith, it is the only life of holiness; and unbelief is the mother of all apostasy. When God would persuade Abraham to sincere and singular godliness, he doth it by offering him sure footing for his faith: "I am God All-sufficient," or the Almighty God; "walk before me, and be thou perfect;"[2] knowing that, unless his faith were firm, his steps could never be even.... Faith is one of the best antidotes against the poison of profaneness, and one of the greatest helps to holiness. None are more faithful to God than they who have most faith in God....

1. [Faith] killeth sin. If the pulse of a Christian's hand or life beat uneven, it is because his faith which is his heart doth falter. This is the shield of the soul, which secures it against all assaults and dangers.... Faith clears up the understanding, and scattereth the mists of error. The presence of this sun disperseth those clouds. Faith secureth the heart from evil purposes. It is the besom that sweepeth out such dust, and keeps the heart clean.[3] Faith entertaineth the

---

1. Swinnock, *Christian Man's Calling*, 3:96–97, 99, 103–106, 108–109.

2. Genesis 17:1.

3. Acts 15:9.

King of saints into the heart; it sets him on the throne, and these traitors fly before him. His presence makes these rebels to hide their heads. Who ever could find in his heart to hug sin, whilst he was viewing, by faith, his bleeding Saviour! Faith secureth the hand from evil practices. The martyrs chose the flames rather than the denial of their Master, and all because of their faith.... Faith ingrafts the soul into Christ, and into the fellowship of his death, by which "the old man is crucified, and the body of sin destroyed, that henceforth we should not serve sin."[4] For therefore did Christ bear our sins in his body on the tree, that we might become dead to sin.[5]

Faith enableth the soul to conquer sin, by enabling it to overcome three grand provocations to sin: the world, the flesh, and the wicked one. There is neither of these enemies but faith hath wounded mortally. (1) Faith enableth to overcome the world. The world, indeed, hath conquered millions.... Unbelief sets a man below, here on earth, and so the things of heaven are little in his eye; but faith soars aloft, it carrieth the Christian up to heaven, and then the whole earth is but a small spot in the eye.... (2) Faith enableth the Christian to conquer Satan. Though the wicked one be full of power and policy, yet faith makes him flee like a coward....[6] The wild bull, say naturalists, cannot endure a red colour, therefore the hunter putteth on red garments, and standeth before a tree, which the bull runneth against with all his might, and the hunter

---

4. Romans 6:5–8.

5. 1 Peter 2:24.

6. James 4:7; 1 Peter 5:9.

stepping aside, his horns stick fast in the tree, whereby he is taken. The Christian, by faith in the blood of Christ overcometh those infernal spirits who thought to overcome him. This is the only holy water that will fright away the devil.... (3) Faith enableth to conquer the flesh.... A traitor in a bedchamber, is much more dangerous than one in open arms against us in the field. A snake in the bosom, is like to do more hurt than one under the grass; partly in that it knoweth our minds exactly, and so can temper its poison suitable to our palates; but faith can discover its secret conspiracies, and prevent their execution. Though it dig its mines never so closely, and covertly, and craftily, faith will find them out, and countermine them.

2. Faith enableth, as to die to sin, so to live to God. The life of holiness doth so much depend on faith, that it is said to consist wholly in it. The just shall live by his faith. Though he cannot live by sense, that upon which he lives being invisible; nor by reason, because his food is supernatural; yet he can live by faith, and make a good living of it too. As the body lives by the soul, so religion lives by faith. A mortal wound in faith, lets out the heart blood of all holiness. It is faith that actuates and animates the new creature. Faith puts him upon high designs, and holy enterprises, for God and his own soul. David saith, "I believe, therefore have I spoken." It may be said of a Christian, he believeth, therefore he speaks so much of God, for God, and to God. He believeth the unquestionable certainty, incomparable excellency, and eternity of that reward which is set before him, and therefore he prayeth, and watcheth, and readeth,

and heareth, and denieth himself, and worketh night and day that he may attain it....

It is by faith that prayer becomes so prevelant.... It is by faith that Scripture is so powerful.... It is by faith that the Lord's Supper becomes so nourishing and strengthening.... It is by faith that crosses are turned into comforts, and afflictions into mercies.... It is by faith that water is turned into wine, temporal mercies into spiritual advantages.... It is by faith that men are so fruitful in their lives,[7] and cheerful in their deaths.[8] O reader, above all thy gettings, get faith, and above all thy keepings, keep faith; for it must be faith that must keep thee from falling in an hour of temptation, and from fainting in an hour of persecution.... Let thy great work be to secure thy faith; if that be whole, all will be well....

---

7. Hebrews 11:32.
8. Romans 8:37–39.

33

Set God Always before Your Eyes[1]

If thou wouldst exercise thyself to godliness, set God always before thine eyes. Subjects will carry themselves handsomely and loyally when they are before their sovereign: they who walk before God, will be upright. His eye is the best marshall to keep the soul in a comely order. Let thine eye be ever on him, whose eye is ever on thee.[2] Seneca[3] persuaded his friend Lucilius, for the keeping him within compass, to imagine that some grave man, as Laelius, did still look upon him. Reader, couldst thou walk ever as in God's presence, thou wouldst keep close to his precepts. Consider, therefore, that in all places, in all companies, at all times, the eye of God is on thee, and he takes exact notice of all thy thoughts, words, and actions; that he knoweth thy natural parts.... There is no drawing a curtain between God and thee; he seeth through and through, far more perfectly than thou canst the clearest crystal....

---

1. Swinnock, *Christian Man's Calling,* 3:109, 112.

2. Proverbs 15:3.

3. Lucius Annaeus Seneca (4 BC– 65 AD) was a Roman moralist. Swinnock finds so much in Seneca's thought, corresponding to his own, that he refers to him as a "Christian heathen." *Christian Man's Calling*, 1:38, 69, 306; 2:10, 149; 3:227.

Hugh Latimer (1485–1555)

There is a story of Bishop Latimer,[4] that he having in a sermon at court much displeased the king, (Henry VIII), was commanded to preach again the next Lord's day, and to recant his former sermon. According to appointment, he cometh up, and prefaceth to his sermon in this manner: Hugh Latimer, dost thou know this day to whom thou art to speak? Even to the high and mighty monarch, the king's most excellent majesty, who can take away thy life if thou offendest; therefore take heed how thou speakest a word which may displease; but, (as if recalling to himself, he proceeded), Hugh, Hugh, dost thou know from whom thou comest, upon whose message thou art sent, and who it is that is present with thee, and beholdeth all thy ways? Even that almighty God who can cast body and soul into hell for ever; therefore look about thee, and be sure thou deliverest thy message faithfully. And so he went to his text, and confirmed what he had spoken the day before, and urged it with more vehemency than ordinary. The eye of God, as of the sun, will call the Christian to his work. Those countries that are governed by viceroys seldom flourish or thrive so well as those kingdoms where the prince is present in person. Conscience, God's viceroy, may much quicken a Christian to holiness; but God the prince himself much more. "I have kept thy precepts," saith David, "for all my ways are before thee."[5]

---

4. Hugh Latimer (1485–1555) was Bishop of Worcester. Because of his Protestant convictions, he was burned at the stake during the reign of Bloody Mary.

5. Psalm 119:168.

34

Watch over Yourself Continually[1]

If thou wouldst exercise thyself to godliness, watch over thyself continually. This spiritual watchfulness is the main guard of the soul, which, if once called off, we lie open to the shot of every enemy. This, like one of the Nethinims,[2] must stand continually porter at the door of our hearts, God's temple, to keep out whatsoever is unclean. Watchfulness is a diligent observation of ourselves in all things, and at all times, that we may please God always.... He who watcheth not is led about, like one in his natural sleep, by any temptation, he knoweth not how or whither. When the wolves in the fable once prevailed with the sheep to part with the dogs, they soon devoured them. If Satan can but get men to forego this means of their safety, he will soon make them his prey. The old world was drowned in sleep before they were drowned in water. Sodom and Gomorrah were secure when they were destroyed by fire....

Watch against sin, against all sin. The gardener doth not only watch over his flowers, to water and cherish them, but also watcheth all weeds, to pluck and root them up. Take heed lest there be any root of

---

1. Swinnock, *Christian Man's Calling*, 3:113, 116–119.

2. See Ezra 2:43, 58, 70; 7:7, 24; 8:17, 20; Nehemiah 3:26, 31; 7:46, 60, 73; 10:28; 11:3, 21.

bitterness.... It is vain for a captain to guard one gate of a castle, to prevent the enemy's entering there, if he leave another open, when the whole fort is beleaguered and surrounded with mortal enemies.

Watch especially against thine own sin. If a man have many wounds, whereof one is more dangerous than the rest, being near a vital part, though he will be mindful and careful of all, yet he will have a special care of that which is most dangerous. A Christian must watch against all sin, all soul diseases, but principally against his own sin—that disease which is most dangerous; as a wise governor will have a special eye upon that particular person in his garrison whom he knoweth to be a traitor.

Watch for the doing of good; for seasons of prayer, and hearing, and Christian communion. The countryman watcheth for the bell ringing on the market-day, when the sacks will be opened, that he may buy food for himself and his family.... An opportunity of worshipping God is a jewel; the Christian may well watch to take it up.

Watch in duties. The child must be watched at school, or he will play and toy, instead of getting his lesson. The heart must be watched in an ordinance, or it will wander wholly from the business in hand....[3] The Bible will drop out of the sleeper's hand, and prayer is a wrestling with God, which is not a work to be done nodding....

Watch after duties.... When the garden is dressed, and the seed is sown in it, we must watch it lest hogs get into it, and root up all. Satan thinks to take the

---

3. Colossians 4:2.

Martin Bucer (1491–1551)

Christian at an advantage, after the duty is over; and though he could not beat him in the fight, yet to do it when the saint hath laid by his weapons....

Watch thy senses. These are the *Cinque Ports*,[4] as one calls them, of the *Isle of man*, which, if not well garrisoned will let in strangers and disturbers of our peace. At these havens much of Satan's lading is taken in. Job made a covenant with his eyes;[5] he would not suffer them to gad and gaze at random, lest they should return defiled.... Shut up the five windows—i.e., guard the five senses, that the whole house may be full of light....

Watch your affections. If those waves be tempestuous, they will cast up much foam and froth, mire and dirt. He had need to make a strong wall, that would keep these raging waters within their bounds.

Watch your tongues. The sea hath not more need of banks to keep it in, than the tongue with a bridle. The tongue is compared to a sword, to a razor, both which are keen weapons, and must be handled warily....[6]

Watch your hearts. The heart is the forge, the spring of life, and a wound there is mortal. Keep thy heart with all diligence...out of it are the issues of life. Watch over all things, watch in all things. This voice, saith Bucer,[7] should always sound in our ears, Watch, watch....

---

4. i.e., five doors.

5. Job 31:1.

6. Psalm 39:1.

7. Martin Bucer (1491–1551) was a German Reformer. He spent some time in England during the reign of Edward VI. Swinnock gives the reference as Bucer in *Mark 8*.

He that watcheth, with Christ, the short hour of his life, shall be counted worthy to reign with him in his kingdom for ever. Sion, which is frequently put for the church of God, signifieth a watch-tower, because from that hill a man might see the Holy Land, and all the countries thereabout; but the spiritual signification of it may be this, that all the members of God's church must be like soldiers in a watch-tower, observing who cometh in and who goeth out, lest traitors should steal into the fort of the heart undiscovered.

35

---••◦••---

Think Often of Your Dying Day[1]

If thou wouldst exercise thyself to godliness, think often of thy dying day, and of what price and value godliness will be to thee at such a time. There are few thoughts more terrible or more profitable than death. Hence it is that God commands man so often to remember his latter end, because the meditation of it is so gainful to him.... If thou wouldst make religion thy business and main work, think often and seriously of thy death and departure of this world. He that guides and steers the ship aright, sits in the stern or hindermost part of it. He that would order his works, his way, according to God, must be frequent in the mediation of his end. The end of his days must be at the end of all his thoughts....

It is worthy our observation, that those who are greatest strangers to death are most familiar with the works of darkness. No place abounds more in wolves, no person in wickedness, than where this mastiff is wanting.... The further we drive death from our thoughts, the nearer we draw to sin. They who fancy their foe to be very far off, will not prepare and make ready to fight....

He who seeth death at his door, will be most diligent about his duty: a serious consideration of the

---

1. Swinnock, *Christian Man's Calling*, 3:119–124, 126.

death of the body will be a sovereign though a sharp medicine to kill the body of death.... Who would make his belly, his gut, his god, who considereth that every meal may be his last, or that thinketh his dainty diet, his fine fare, doth but provide a greater feast for worms? Who would give way to sinful wantons, who believeth that whilst he is unloading his lust, God may put a period to his life? He that is high in conceit of himself, little dreameth how low he must shortly be laid. Who would be proud of that body which shall ere long see corruption, become such a noisome, loathsome carcase, that the nearest and dearest relations will not endure the sight or scent of it? He who loveth the world inordinately, forgetteth that he may leave it suddenly, and must leave it certainly....

Those who are most mindful of their deaths, are most faithful in their lives. Job was eminent in grace, because Job was daily conversing with his grave. All the days of his appointed time he waited till his change came.[2] That servant will follow his work most and best, who expecteth his master's coming every moment....

Some say that nothing in this world is so strong as death, because it subdueth the mighty, it conquereth the greatest conquerors, it overcometh all. Sure I am, that death hath great force and power over men's souls, as well as over their bodies. The thought of it hath raised some to a spiritual life. The consideration of death hath also caused others to live much in a little space; when they have seen the sun of their lives near setting, and the night of their deaths approach-

---

2. Job 14:14.

ing, they have in the day followed their work with the greater diligence. None will work so hard as they who think themselves near their everlasting homes....

O reader, if thou wilt but often wind up this weight of thine approaching death, it would keep thy soul in a quick, spiritual, and regular motion at all times. As ashes preserve fire, and keep coals from going out, so the thought that we shall ere long be turned into ashes will preserve the fire of grace alive and in action.

36

Mind a Daily Performance
of Sacred Duties[1]

If thou wouldst exercise thyself to godliness, mind a daily performance of sacred duties. He that hath nothing of his own whereupon to live, must be frequently fetching in provision from the shops or market where it is to be had. The Christian's life is maintained, not by himself, but by what he receiveth from God; not that we are sufficient of ourselves, our sufficiency is of God; therefore there is a necessity of daily converse with God by holy ordinances, and of waiting at his gate; as the beggar, who hath neither a bit of bread, nor a penny to buy any, at the rich man's door for supply. Our spiritual strength is like Israel's manna, rained down daily; we are kept by a divine power, and allowed but from hand to mouth, that we might continually depend on, and resort to, the Lord Jesus for our allowance....

Sacred duties are as needful every day for our souls as food and raiment for our bodies. The body must continually be repaired with nourishment, because it is continually consumed by our natural heat. Yesterday's bread will not keep the labourer today in strength and vigour to go through with his work; he

---

1. Swinnock, *Christian Man's Calling*, 3:126–131.

must have new diet, or he cannot hold out. Friend, I must bespeak thee, as the angel to Elijah, Up and eat, for the journey is too great for thee.[2] Up and be doing in prayer, and Scripture, and holy ordinances, that thou mayest feed and receive spiritual nourishment; for otherwise the business of exercising thyself to god-liness, the duties required of thee to be performed, the graces to be exercised, the temptations to be resisted, the deadly enemies to be conquered will be too hard for thee, the journey will be too great for thee.... The more a Christian mindeth divine ordinances, in obedience to God's precept, and affiance on God's promise, the more strength he shall receive to conquer his spiritual adversaries, and to discharge the several duties incumbent on him. The truth is, our religious life, our heavenly flame, is like a straw fire to malt, which must constantly be tended and fed with fuel, or it will go out.... As trees being well ordered with skill and diligence, they become abundantly fruitful; but being left to themselves, without culture and care, they bring forth little fruit or no fruit. So Christians, by a diligent use of means, abound in the fruits of righteousness, but neglecting ordinances, they decline and decay....

When Christians grow careless of duties, and neglect their closets, it is no wonder that they decline in their spiritual stocks.... There is no growing in grace and holiness, but by conversing with heaven.

---

2. 1 Kings 19:5–7.

37

Meditate Much upon the Day of Judgment[1]

If thou wouldst exercise thyself to godliness meditate much upon the day of judgment. They will prepare themselves best to the battle who always hear the sound of the last trump in their ears.... Could the Christian but, with Jerome, hear the sound of the last trumpet in his ears at all times, it would encourage him in his spiritual warfare, and enable him to fight manfully, and to cause the enemies of his salvation to flee before him. He who can frequently, by faith, view the Judge sitting on his throne of glory, hear the last trumpet sounding; behold the dead raised, the books opened, the godly examined by the covenant of grace, all their duties, graces, services, sufferings publicly declared, approved, and rewarded; the wicked tried by the law of works; all their natural defilements, actual transgressions in thought, word, and deed which ever they were guilty of, with their crimson bloody circumstances openly revealed, their persons righteously sentenced to the vengeance of the eternal fire, and that sentence speedily, without the least favour or delay, executed on them, will surely loathe sin as that which brings him certain shame and

---

1. Swinnock, *Christian Man's Calling*, 3:131–133, 135, 138–140.

torment, and follow after holiness, which will be his undoubted credit and comfort at that day....

(1) Consider the holiness of the Judge. He is the holy Jesus. He loveth righteousness, and hateth iniquity. What will the ungodly sinner do when he shall be judged by the holy Saviour? Who can stand before this holy God?....[2] (2) Consider the strictness of his proceedings. Every thought, word, and action shall be revealed, examined, and weighed in the balance of the sanctuary: "There is nothing hid that shall not be revealed, nor secret that shall not be made known."[3] The thoughts of thy heart shall then be as visible as the features of thy face....[4] (3) Consider the weight of the sentence. It is called eternal judgment, because the sentence then pronounced shall never be reversed, but stand for ever.... (4) Consider the felicity of the godly at that day. Oh, with what joy will they lift up their heads when that day of their redemption is come! This life is the day of their oppression and persecution, but that day will be the day of their redemption.... (5) To affrighten thee from sin, consider the misery of sinners at that day. It is called the day of perdition of ungodly men. Sin will be sin indeed at that day.... Ah who can dwell in everlasting burnings? Who can abide devouring flames? Who can imagine the shame that will cover their faces, the horror that will fill their hearts, the terrors, the tortures, and torments that must seize them for ever?....

---

2. 1 Samuel 6:20.

3. Mark 4:22.

4. Romans 2:16.

Reader, at this day think much of that day of judgment; hereby thou wilt be stirred up to judge thyself, to repent of sin, to ensure an interest in Christ the Judge, to keep a good conscience, and so to think, speak, and act as one that must be judged by the law of liberty.[5]

---

5. Acts 3:19; 17:31; 24:16; 1 Corinthians 11:31; James 2:12; 2 Peter 3:11.

38

Call Yourself to an Account[1]

If thou wouldst exercise thyself to godliness, call thyself often to an account. This is a special help to holiness: "I considered my ways, and turned my feet to thy testimonies," saith David.[2] A man that goeth out of his way will continue wandering, if his mind be occupied about other things, and he consider not what he is doing, and whither he is going. The Christian that is careless of his carriage, and seldom compareth his heart and life with the divine commands, to observe how they agree or disagree, will never order his conversation aright. When a clock is out of order we take it to pieces, and search where the fault lieth, knowing that one wheel amiss may hinder the going of the whole clock. Our hearts are every day out of order; our work must be to take them to pieces by examination, and to see where the great fault is....

Reader, if thou wouldst walk closely with God, and keep even with him, reckon daily with him, call thyself to a strict scrutiny: What do I? How live I? Where am I? Is the work I do warrantable by the word or no? Is my life the life of faith, of holiness, or no? Am I in God's way, under his protection, or no? Have I truth of grace, the power of godliness, or do

---

1. Swinnock, *Christian Man's Calling*, 3:140–141, 144–145.
2. Psalm 119:59.

I please myself with the form of it? Do I thrive and increase in grace, or do I decay and decline? Suppose I were to die this night, what ground have I to hope for heaven? What assurance that I shall escape the power and rage of frightful devils? What evidences have I that I am a new creature, engrafted into Christ, and thereby entitled to life and bliss? Thus feel the pulse of thy soul, inquire into its state, visit it often, and see how it doth.

Call thyself to an account for thy sins; let heart and life sins, open and private sins, omissions, commissions, personal, relative, be all reckoned for.... The heart is like a ditch, into which filth is continually running; and therefore it behoveth thee, by examination, to be always emptying it....

Call thyself to an account daily, for thy mercies; ask thyself, How much am I indebted to my God? What privative, what positive mercies do I partake of? What old, what new, what night, what day, mercies? What mercies at home, what abroad? What personal, what domestical, what national, mercies do I enjoy, or am a sharer in? What bodily, what spiritual, mercies do I receive? What time, what talents, have I to trade with and reckon for? This will help the soul to be speedy and hearty in thankfulness....

39

Avoid the Occasions of Sin[1]

If thou wouldst exercise thyself to godliness, avoid the occasions of sin. He that would avoid the commission of sin, must avoid the occasions of sin. If we would not fall down the hill, we must beware of coming near the brow of it. Keep thee far from an evil matter....

He that carrieth always along with him a heart ready to break out into a flame, prone to all wickedness, had need to take heed of those bellows that will help to blow up the fire. I more fear, saith Luther, that which is within me, than that which is from without.... The best heart is like a flint; there is fire in it, though it doth not appear; occasion is the steel that fetcheth it forth, which, being let alone, would be quiet. Bees in winter, being sensible of their weakness, keep their hives, and will not expose themselves to the sharp air and bitter frosts, lest thereby they sicken and die. Alas! how weak is man, how unable to resist the occasions of sin!—no more than the hound can forbear pursuing the hare before his eyes, and therefore it concerns him to avoid them. A candle newly extinguished, will quickly be lighted again. Powder meeting with a lighted match presently takes fire....

Reader, as thou wouldst shun sin in the action, shun it in the occasion; remember thou carriest thatch

---

1. Swinnock, *Christian Man's Calling*, 3:145–148.

Martin Luther (1483–1546)

about thee, and therefore oughtest to avoid the least sparks. A little wind will drive a ship with the stream and tide, and a small temptation may carry thee that way which thy wicked heart inclines thee. A little pulling will draw a strong man whither he is willing to go; it is safest, therefore, to be out of harm's way, and the greatest magnanimity to fly from the sight of such an enemy as sin is. He hath most true courage who makes a timely retreat before he be wounded.

40

Walk Humbly with Your God[1]

If thou wouldst exercise thyself to godliness, walk humbly with thy God. A tree, the more deeply it is rooted, the more it groweth under ground, the more upward in fruitfulness. The Christian will find that, by growing in humility, he shall thrive in godliness. He that turneth his eyes upward, is ready to stumble at every rub that lieth in his way; but he that looketh downward, seeth and avoideth those stones. A proud man is like a little man with a high-heeled shoe, raised thereby, in his own conceit, above others of the same rank, but it fits him with many a fall. The proud person giveth not glory to God, and therefore must not expect that God should give grace to him; but the humble man honoureth God and sanctifieth his name, and sets the crown on his head, and so may expect, because God hath promised, that God should honour him, and sanctify his soul....

Alas! What is man? What hath man that he should be proud? He is but enlivened dust, moving earth, refined clay, that which beasts trample under their feet. He hath nothing that is good but what he hath received. He lives wholly upon the alms and charity of another. A proud heart and a beggar's purse do not agree. As he is a sinner, he is more vile

---

1. Swinnock, *Christian Man's Calling*, 3:148, 150–151.

and base, more noisome and loathsome, than any toad, or snake, or serpent; and hath he any reason to be proud? Reader, be clothed with humility; learn of thy Redeemer, for he was meek and lowly of heart. Though he thought it not robbery to be equal with God, yet he "made himself of no reputation, and took upon him the form of a servant."[2]

When pride cometh, then cometh a fall. As a wrestler, if he can lift his fellow from the ground, quickly gives him a fall; so the devil, if he can lift up with pride, doubts not but to throw them.... Angels, Adam, David, Hezekiah, Peter, and many others in Scripture, confirm the wise man's proverb, "Pride goeth before a fall."[3] Trees that are set on mountains are easily shaken and torn up by the roots when stormy winds arise. Indeed, it is no wonder that a proud man should fall into sin, for he relieth on his own strength which is but a broken reed. Peter had not fallen so foully if he had not undertaken to stand upon his own legs, which were too weak to bear his weight. But before honour is humility. The lower the foundation, the higher the building.

---

2. Philippians 2:7–8.
3. Proverbs 16:18.

41

Suppress Sin in the Beginning[1]

If thou wouldst exercise thyself to godliness, suppress sin in the beginning. This foul bird is easiest killed in the egg. When a fire is first broke out in a chimney, it may with much less labour be quenched than when it hath seized the timber in the house. What small beginnings had those fires which have conquered stately palaces, and turned famous cities into ruinous heaps! A hair is but a little thing, yet some have been choked with it.... Passion at the first kindling may be quenched; but if let alone, sends such a smoke into the understanding, which thickens into a cloud, and hinders us from the sight of ourselves and our duties. The tree may soon be pulled up before it hath taken root, but then it may be too hard for the strongest man. A prick with a pin or a thorn, being let alone, hath sometimes caused the cutting off of a limb, nay, the loss of life....

Sin increaseth by degrees:[2] first it surpriseth the heart in a thought, then it stealeth into the affections for approbation, then the affections plead with the will for its consent, and then that commandeth the act of it, and frequent acts cause a habit, and custom in sin causeth despair, despair causeth men to defend

---

1. Swinnock, *Christian Man's Calling*, 3:152–153.

2. James 1:14–15.

sin, their defence of sin a boasting and glorying in it, and the next step is hell. Sin is therefore fitly by the prophet compared to a chain, for one link draweth another.

As the ivy by little and little creepeth upon the oak, till at last it doth destroy it, so doth sin cling about the soul, and by degrees overrun and undo it. When the water begins to freeze, it will hardly bear a pennyweight; let it alone a little longer and it will bear a shilling, then a pound weight, then a man, then a horse, then cart and load and all. As the cloud which Elijah's servant saw was at first no bigger than a man's hand, but afterwards it spread till it covered the heavens.[3] Peter first denieth his Master, then sweareth, then curseth, and forsweareth himself.[4] Cain first harbours envious thoughts of his brother, then murdereth him in his heart, then kills him with his hand, then quarrelleth with God and despaireth.[5] There is no staying, when we are once down the hill, till we come to the bottom. If this giant of sin get in but a limb, he will quickly get in his whole body. Wanton thoughts, if not stifled, bring forth actual uncleanness. Sin is like water—if we give it the least way, run it will in spite of us. If we get not the conquest over it in its infancy, we shall not overcome it when it is brought to maturity. He that cannot put out a spark will be much more unable to put out a flame. The smallest of these twigs will prove thorny bushes, if not timely stubbed up.

---

3. 1 Kings 18:44.

4. Matthew 26:73–75.

5. Genesis 4:1–16.

42

Study the Knowledge of God[1]

If thou wouldst exercise thyself to godliness, study the knowledge of God. It is ignorance of God that is the origin of all sin. Did men know the sad fruits of his fury, they durst not by sin provoke him. Did men know the sweetness of his favour, they would do, they would suffer anything to please him. It is in the mist of ignorance that they lose their way, and wander from him who is the chiefest good. The devil is bound in chains of darkness, and so are all his children.

They who know God most, love him most, and fear him most, and trust him most. It is life spiritual, and the seed of life eternal, to know thee the only true God, and Jesus Christ, whom thou hast sent.[2] All godliness, all grace, is seminally in the knowledge of God, and floweth from it....

They who know the infiniteness and immensity of his being, cannot but despise all things for him, esteem all things as nothing to him, as nothing without him; look on the whole creation as less than nothing in comparison of him....

They who know the power of God cannot but fear him, and stand in awe of his presence and threatenings. They fear him who is able to cast soul and body

1. Swinnock, *Christian Man's Calling*, 3:153–156, 158.

2. John 17:3.

into hell.[3] They will depend on him, because there is no want which the Almighty cannot supply, no weakness which he cannot remove, no danger which he cannot prevent or support in....

They who know the eternity of God, will choose him before temporal vanities. What are the pleasures of sin for a season in his eye, who seeth the pleasures at God's right hand for evermore? What are the honours on earth to him who knoweth the eternal weight of glory? What are the temporal relations in comparison of the everlasting Father? Nay, what is natural life to eternal life?....

They who know the wisdom of God will submit to his providences, and acquiesce in all his dispensations. He is wise in heart, his understanding is infinite, and he knoweth what is best for thee, and me, and all others, and therefore there is all the reason of the world why I should rest in his will, and be satisfied in his pleasure....

They who know the faithfulness of God will credit his word, and make him the object of their hope and faith: "They that know thy name will trust thee."[4] His truth commandeth our trust. We will rely on faithful men, who will not lie; but the Christian seeth infinitely more reason to rely on the faithful God, who cannot lie.

They who know the mercy, and love, and goodness of God, will love, and admire, and trust, and praise him. The knowledge of his love to us will call out our love to him, as one that deserves it, being

---

3. Matthew 10:28; Hebrews 12:27–28.
4. Psalm 9:10.

infinitely amiable in himself, and the more deserving of our love for his love to such loathsome ones as we are....

They who know the holiness of God will sanctify him in their approaches to him, and walk humbly and watchfully with him. They know that sin is loathsome to him, because contrary to his holy nature, and therefore they hate it....

They who know the anger of God will stand in awe, and not sin. They know that God is not to be mocked; for it is a fearful thing to fall into the hands of the living God, for our God is a consuming fire.[5] They know his fury is terrible, intolerable; none can abide it, no sinner can avoid it. Therefore, they hate sin, the object of it, and fly to Christ, who delivereth from it.

Oh what a work, a gracious sanctifying work, doth the knowledge of God make in the soul! It makes the understanding to esteem him above all, the will to choose him before all, the affections to desire him, to delight in him, more than all; the whole man to seek him, to serve him, to honour and praise him beyond all in heaven and earth....

O reader, be confident of this, the more thou knowest of the excellencies of God, the more thou wilt prize his Son, submit to his Spirit, crucify the flesh, condemn the world, fear to offend him, study to please him, the more holy thou wilt be in all manner of conversation....

Reader, be persuaded, therefore, to study this knowledge of God; think no labour too much for it; pray, and read, and hear, and confer, and mourn that

---

5. Hebrews 12:29.

thou mayest know God. Believe it, it is a jewel that will pay thee well for all thy pains. Incline thine ear unto wisdom, and apply thy heart unto understanding. Yea, if thou criest after knowledge, and liftest up thy voice for understanding; if thou seekest her as silver, and searchest for her as for hid treasures, then shalt thou understand the fear of the Lord, and find the knowledge of God: "For the Lord giveth wisdom, and out of his mouth cometh knowledge and understanding."[6]

---

6. Proverbs 2:2–6.

43

Labour to Get a Contented Frame of Heart[1]

If thou wouldst exercise thyself to godliness, labour to get a contented frame of heart. A settled, fixed frame of heart as to all outward occurrences, is like ballast[2] to a ship, which will help it to sail trim in all waters; whereas a discontented spirit is as a light, small boat in the ocean, tossed about with every blast, and always in danger of drowning....

Whilst we are in this world we must expect various winds—some sharp, some warm, some nipping, some refreshing, some with us, some against us; and unless we are prepared for all by a holy pliableness, we shall be injured by every one. Every strong wind, whether with us or against us, will be ready to overturn us if we want this ballast. There is no condition in this life so blessed as to afford the perfection of content; and yet there is no estate in this life so wretched but a Christian may be contented with it. If thou hast as much as thou wantest, thou hast as much as in reason thou desirest, and therefore hast cause to be contented....

---

1. Swinnock, *Christian Man's Calling*, 3:158–164.

2. I.e., weight.

He that can bring his heart to an even poise in all providences will avoid many temptations, and escape many snares in which others are entangled. The want of this renders many a man's life as unserviceable to God as uncomfortable to himself. The discontented person, like the sea, is seldom seen without storms and tempests. A small matter puts him out of order and joint, and so unfits him for spiritual actions. As hot iron, the smallest drop sets him a hissing; like a ruffled skein of silk, every way taken to compose him entangleth him. Discontent, like ink poured into a bottle of water, turns all into blackness. O friend, beware of it!

It hinders from praying. A discontented man will rather pour out his passions than any sober prayers before the Lord.

It hinders examining ourselves.... Though the heart, when calm and contented, may shew us the face and features of our souls, yet if muddied by discontent they cannot do it.[3]

It hinders from hearing. The noise of passion drowns the voice of the preacher. Men must with meekness receive the ingrafted word, if they desire it should save their souls.[4]

When a fountain is troubled, there can not water be drawn out of it but what is filthy and unsavoury. When a person is discontented, all his duties are distasteful and unacceptable to God. Therefore, Christ more than once dissuades his disciples from it: "Let

---

3. Psalm 55:4–5; John 14:27.

4. James 1:21.

not your hearts be troubled. Let not your heart be troubled, neither let it be afraid"....[5]

There be several thoughts which may quiet and compose the heart in all occurrents. (1) That infinite wisdom ordaineth whatsoever befalleth me, and the present condition that I am in is ever best for me.... (2) That the smallest mercy is above my merits. If my condition be not so good as I desire, yet it is better than I deserve.... (3) That, be our estate as low as it will, it is better than we brought with us into the world.... (4) That a better condition might and would make me worse. If I were mounted high in the world, I should be like the flag at the top of the mast, more liable to storms and winds.... (5) That others, who are better than I, and more holy, are worse for this world, and suffer more hardships.... (6) That all shall work for my good.[6] The saint is sure to thrive by his sufferings.... (7) That the more I repine, the worse I make my condition. A discontented man, like one in a barrel of pikes, which way soever he turns, he finds something that pricks. (8) That the examples of others may have some prevalency with us. Abraham, Moses, and Paul were eminent for this grace.... (9) That the Lord is righteous in all his ways, and holy in all his works. He doeth thee no wrong, he cannot do thee any wrong.... (10) That God is gracious and good in all his dealings with thee....

---

5. John 14:1, 27.
6. Romans 8:28.

44

━━ ❋ ━━

Take Heed of Those Things
that Will Hinder You[1]

Lastly, If thou wouldst exercise thyself to godliness, take heed of those things that will hinder thee therein. As if a man would have his trees to thrive, he must not only open the earth sometimes and mind its watering, but also lop off superfluous branches; and as a gardener, if he would have his herbs and flowers to flourish, must be sure to keep his banks and beds well weeded, as well as dunged and watered; so if thou wouldst thrive and flourish in godliness, there is a necessity of avoiding what is hurtful to it, as well as of using what is helpful.

There be several things which will keep a Christian from the exercise of his holy calling....

1. Avoid evil company.... Expect not that the flowers of thy graces should flourish unless these weeds be removed from them. He that walketh in the rain must expect to be wet; he that walketh in the sun must expect to be tanned; and he that walks among polluting persons must expect to be polluted.

2. Take heed of idleness. An idle man is like a heap of dry straw, quickly fired by the sparks of

---

1. Swinnock, *Christian Man's Calling*, 3:164–166.

Satan's temptations....[2] Whilst the oyster lieth gaping against the sun, he is devoured by the crabfish. Whilst the Christian lieth lazying on the bed of idleness, he is a prey to Satan....

3. Love not the world. The thorns of the world hinder the growth of the good seed of grace.... It is hard for the periwinkle in the sea to swim, because of the house on her back; it is impossible for them to swim heavenward who have the world, not on their backs, but in their hearts. The more thou delightest in this world, the more thou wilt neglect the other world....

4. Allow thyself in no known sin. This is like a thief used to the shop, which will steal away all thy gains, and keep thee assuredly from thriving in thy heavenly calling. There is no possibility of making religion thy business without the gracious concurrence of the Holy Spirit; he it is that must lay the foundation, rear up the building, and perfect what he beginneth; but thou canst not expect his company or assistance if thou harbourest any corruption in thy heart.

---

2. Proverbs 18:19; 2 Thessalonians 3:10–11; 1 Timothy 5:13.

SECTION SEVEN

The Motives
to Godliness

45

———— ⋗•⟨•⟩•⟨⟩ ————

Consider the Vanity
of all Other Exercises[1]

The wise man begins his Ecclesiastes with vanity of vanities, all is vanity; and after a large and exact demonstration thereof, makes this use, and ends his book with, "Hear the conclusion of the whole matter: Fear God and keep his commandments; for this is the whole duty of man." It may be, reader, thou takest much pains and spendest much time; thou risest early, and sittest up late; and wasteth thy body, and wearest out thy strength; and toilest and moilest about the things of this life; but alas! to what purpose? To what profit?.... If the word of truth, and the God for whom it is impossible to lie, may be believed, all the things of this life separated from godliness are lying vanities, broken cisterns, ashes, lies, wind, vanity of vanities, and things of naught....[2]

The vanity of other labours will appear in that all other things are unsuitable, deceitful, unsatisfying, vexatious, and uncertain.

1. Unsuitable to the soul. Gold is unsuitable to hunger, food to the sick, honour to the weary; so

---

1. Swinnock, *Christian Man's Calling*, 3:167, 169–172, 175.

2. Jonah 2:8; Jeremiah 2:13; 1 Samuel 12:21; Hosea 10:13; 12:1; Ecclesiastes 1:2; Habakkuk 2:13.

are all the comforts of this life to the soul. What is an earthly treasure to the poor in spirit? What is the best physic-garden to a wounded conscience? What are all the dainties on the table of the creation to one that is hungry and thirsty after the righteousness of Christ, and the grace of the Spirit? Bodily things are not suitable to our spirits, nor temporal substance to an immortal soul....

2. Deceitful. As Jael to Sisera,[3] the world brings forth meat to us in lovely dish, and saith, Come in, my lord, turn in; but she puts her hand to the nail, and her right hand to the workman's hammer. With the hammer she smites foolish Siseras that trust her; she smites off their heads after she hath pierced their temples.... The world, next man's heart, is the greatest cheat and imposter in the world. Like a host, it welcomes us in our inns with smiles and embraces, but kills us in our beds, when we suspect no such matter....

3. Unsatisfying. All these sublunary comforts are but skin-deep. As a mist, they may wet the blade, but leave the root of the corn dry; they may cause a smile in the face, but cannot refresh the heart, or satisfy the soul.... Men think if they could attain to such a degree of honour, or such a quantity of riches or enjoy such brutish pleasures, then they should be satisfied, but they find their thirst after creatures as immoderate as before.... The soul will starve, for all the food which the whole world affordeth it....

4. The things of this world are vexatious. Their sting paineth far more than their honey pleaseth....

---

3. Judges 4:13–22.

All the ways of worldly delights are strewed with net-
tles and briers, so that its greatest darlings are but like
bears robbing a bee-hive, that with much labour get a
little honey, but are soundly stung for their pains....

5. Uncertain. There is no constancy in outward
comforts. As brooks in winter are carried with vio-
lence and run with a mighty stream, flowing over
with abundance of water on every side, when there is
no want nor need of waters; but in the heat of summer
is dried up, when water is scanty and hard to be had;
such is the friendship of the world; it will promise
us many things when we have need of nothing; but
when the wind turns, and afflictions overtake us, it
is like a tree withered for want of sap, and as a ditch
without any water to refresh us....

The plain truth is, the world is the ruin and
destruction of men.... Oh do not spend thy strength
for that which is not bread, but hearken to Christ, and
thou shalt eat that which is good, and thy soul shall
delight thyself in fatness.[4]

---

4. Isaiah 55:3–4.

46

━►═◄(●)►═◄━

Consider the Brevity of Life[1]

He who hath but a little time, and a great task, must work hard, or his work will not be done....

Now, reader, consider how few thy days are. What is your life? even a vapour, a coming and a going, a flood and an ebb, and then thou art in the ocean of eternity. I have read of one, that being asked what life was, was answered answerless; for the party of whom the question was demanded only turned his back and went away. We come into the world, and take a turn or two about in it, and God saith, Return, ye children of men. A little child may number the days of the oldest man. We project high things, and lay foundations for an earthly eternity, but the longest life is less than a drop to that ocean....

It is our shame and misery that our days should be so swift, and we so slack; that our time should be as speedy as a post, or ship, or eagle, and our hearts as slow about our eternal concernments as a snail. Our negligence herein speaks us brutish, and void of common sense. Reason will teach him that followeth its directions, to be most industrious about matters of such importance....

The heathen historian can agree with Scripture in this: Our life passeth away, as a tale that is told;

---

1. Swinnock, *Christian Man's Calling*, 3:175–177.

it matters not much whether it be long or short, but whether it be well or ill.

Surely it concerneth thee, reader, to make religion thy business, and work the work of God, when thine everlasting happiness dependeth on it, and thy time is so short that thou hast to do it in. In the days of Ptolomeus Philopater, when the huge and great anchor of the ship Thalmegos was laid out upon the shore, the children of Alexandria did ride upon the stalk, and crept through the ring of the anchor as if it had been made purposely for their pastime, whereas wise men knew it was appointed for better uses, namely, to stable and make sure the great vessel in storms and tempests.

Truly, so do too many serve time; they play, and toy, and trifle it away, as if God had given it to them for that end; when he who hath but half an eye, as we say, may see that it was given for better purposes, viz., to furnish his soul for his eternal voyage and thereby to help to stablish and fasten him when he shall launch into the stormy ocean.

47

——•(○)•——

Consider the Example of Others[1]

Consider the examples of others, who have wrought hard at this heavenly calling. Cicero[2] tells us, Nothing prevails more with men than similitudes and examples. Indeed, worthy patterns are of great power.... Consider, therefore the prophets and apostles of the Lord, how diligent they were at their duty, how hard they wrought for God.

The great apostle was indefatigably industrious for his soul and his Saviour. Consider him in reference to his outward man, how unwearied was he at his Master's work! and in reference to his inward man, how zealous, how fervent in spirit, serving the Lord! "From Jerusalem to Illyricum I have preached the gospel"....[3]

Reader, think thou hearest the apostle speaking to thee, as once to the Corinthians, "Be ye followers of me, as I am of Christ." How did our blessed Saviour work the work of him that sent him while it was day? He went about doing good. Godliness was his meat and drink: "I have meat to eat which ye know not of. My meat is to do the will of him that sent me, and to

---

1. Swinnock, *Christian Man's Calling*, 3:177–179.

2. Marcus Tullius Cicero (106–43 BC) was a Roman orator.

3. Romans 15:19.

finish his work."[4] He wrought so hard that he forgot to eat his bread, and was taken by his kindred to be mad. It was his sleep and rest....

O reader, let Christ be the copy after which thou wilt write, and the pattern which thou wilt follow, and be a follower of others as they are of Christ Jesus. Did Christ work so hard for thee; did he lose his food, and sleep, and wear out himself, that his strength was dried up like a potsherd, and his heart was melted like wax in the midst of his bowels, and wilt thou spend and be spent for thy Saviour?—I would say for thy own soul; for in serving him thou servest thyself. Think of it when thou art trifling away thy time, and neglecting thy spiritual watch, and dull and dead in holy duties. How eager and earnest, how zealous and sedulous, thy Lord Jesus was in working out thy salvation! He did not play, nor dally about the work of thy redemption, but made it his business, and did what he was called to with all his heart, and soul, and strength.

---

4. John 4:32.

48

---❖ ⭑❖⭑ ❖---

Consider the Excellency
of this Calling[1]

As it is said of God in respect of beings, "Who is like thee, O God? Among all the gods none is to be compared to thee;"[2] so I may say of godliness in respect of callings, What is like thee, O godliness? Amongst all callings none is comparable to thee.

1. It is the most honourable calling. The master that thou art bound to is King of kings, and Lord of lords, the fountain of honour, and Lord of glory; one of whom the greatest princes and potentates of the world hold their crowns and sceptres, to whom they must kneel and do their homage; one to whom the whole creation is less than nothing. The work that thou art employed in is not servile and mean, but high and noble; the worship of the great God, walking and conversing with his blessed Majesty, subduing brutish lusts, living above this beggarly earth, a conversation in heaven, a conflict with, and conquest over, this dreggy flesh and drossy world, and powers of hell, to which the greatest battles and victories of the most valiant warriors that ever drew the sword are worse than

---

1. Swinnock, *Christian Man's Calling*, 3:179, 182, 185, 187, 189–190, 192.

2. Psalm 89:6.

children's play. To conquer our passions is more than to conquer kingdoms.... To subdue our lust, is more than to subdue a thousand cities.... The privileges of this calling and company are eminent. Adoption, remission, growth in grace, divine love, perseverance in holiness, an eternal kingdom, are all contained in the charter granted to this corporation....

2. It is the most comfortable and delightful calling.... Godliness brings more noble and excellent pleasures. Others are puddle-water; those pleasures which godliness giveth are pure and clear streams, such as flow from God himself. There is more sweetness in one drop of the fountain, than in all the waters of the sea. There is more joy, more comfort, in a little communion with God, than in the greatest confluence of creature enjoyments. Augustine saith, How sweet was it to me on a sudden to be without these sweet vanities! Thou, Lord, who art the true sweetness, didst take them from me and enter in thyself, who art more pleasant than all pleasure, and more clear than all light.[3] The world as they say of fairies, deprives of true children, and puts changelings in their room; deprives men of true substantial joy, and gives them shadows in the room; but godliness, on the contrary, deprives of painted poisons, and gives them wholesome and real pleasures....

3. It is the most profitable calling.... Now, reader, if profit will prevail with thee, godliness with contentment is great gain.[4] All the gold of the world is dross, all the diamonds of the world are dirt, all the gains of

---

3. Swinnock gives the reference as *Conf., lib. ix, cap. 1.*
4. 1 Timothy 6:6.

Augustine of Hippo (354–450), printed
by Sandro Botticelli (ca. 1480).

the world are loss, to this gain of godliness…. (1) It is real…its fruit is therefore called substance, in distinction from earthly riches, which are shadows: "I will cause them that love me to inherit substance." (2) It is called also true riches; other riches are feigned…it makes the soul of man truly precious, as it is most serviceable to our last end, and prepareth man for the fruition of God, and also as its reward is unconceivable. The vessel of mercy shall swim in an ocean of glory: "Eye hath not seen, nor ear heard, nor can the heart of man conceive what God hath laid up for them that love him."[5] Its reward is beyond all expression…. (3) It is eternal gain. Other gains are fading, deceitful brooks, dying flowers, withering gourds, and vanishing shadows…. The fear of the Lord is clean, enduring for ever, both in the nature of it, it is incorruptible seed, and in the fruit of it, which is the gift of God, eternal life…. (4) It is certain gain. He that sets up of this trade may be trusted, for none ever brake of this calling. God himself, whose is the earth and the fullness thereof, is bound of them, and hath undertaken for their perseverance, and growth, and gains….

O reader, what an argument is here to provoke thee to piety. Godliness is profitable in all conditions, in all relations, in both worlds. In prosperity, it will be a sun to direct thee; in adversity, a shield to protect thee; in life, it will be thy comfort, and, which is infinitely more, in death, that hour of need, it will be thy enlivening cordial….

---

5. 1 Corinthians 2:9.

Conclusion

A Call to Godliness[1]

If the God upon whom thou livest, by whom thou movest, from whom thou hast thy being, may be heard, thou wilt now wink on the world, crucify the flesh, loathe thyself for thy filth and folly, and devote thy heart and soul to his fear. He commandeth thee by his dominion over thee, and thy obligations to him; he threateneth, promiseth, affrighteth, allureth, and all to make thee mind thy allegiance to him, and the work he hath given thee to do in this world. If thy Saviour, who humbled himself for thy sake, and took upon him the form of a servant, and in thy nature was buffeted, scourged, and crucified, may be heard, then thou wilt immediately take the counsel that is given thee, and turn to the Lord with all thy heart, and loathe thyself for all thine abominations. He pleads with thee most pathetically,[2] presenteth to thee the stripes and wounds which sin caused in his blessed body; the blood which he shed, the ignominy he endured, the agony, the death he suffered and all to satisfy for sin, to make himself Lord both of the dead and living. He tells thee he gave himself for thee, to redeem thee from all iniquity, and to purify thee to himself a peculiar child zealous of good works. If

---

1. Swinnock, *Christian Man's Calling*, 3:195–196.
2. I.e., earnestly and sincerely.

the daily, and nightly, and hourly mercies that thou enjoyest; if the sickness, or pain, or loss, or disgrace, or afflictions which sometimes thou sufferest, may be heard, there would not be so much ado to persuade a wretched creature to be blessed, and an ungodly person to be holy and happy. If the inanimate and irrational creatures, the earth beneath thee, the heavens above thee, the beasts and birds about thee, might be heard, thou wouldst, whilst it is called today, now, after so long a time, attend to the call and command of him, in whose hand is thy life and breath, and follow after holiness, without which thou shalt never see the Lord.[3]

---

3. Hebrews 12:14.

Reading Swinnock

Richard Baxter asks, "What books, especially of theology, should one choose, who for want of money or time can read but few?" That is an excellent question, especially when we factor in the number of books written since Baxter's day! His answer is insightful: "It is not the reading of many books which is necessary to make a man wise or good; but the well reading of a few, could he be sure to have the best."[1] Baxter proceeds to provide a description of the "best" or what he calls "the smallest library that is tolerable." In it, he lists the works of the "affectionate practical English writers," including George Swinnock.[2]

I trust you have tasted something of Swinnock's worth in this small volume. If you are interested in reading more about him, you will be disappointed to learn that there are no biographies available. Apart from my book, *Puritan Spirituality: The Fear of God in the Affective Theology of George Swinnock* (Milton Keynes: Paternoster, 2007), there are no secondary sources dealing with his theology or spirituality. However, if you are interested in reading more by

---

1. Richard Baxter, *A Christian Directory* (1673) in *The Practical Works of Richard Baxter* (London: George Virtue, 1846: rpt., Morgan: Soli Deo Gloria, 2000), 1:731.

2. Baxter, *Christian Directory*, 1:732.

Swinnock, you will be pleased to learn that his works are readily available. Without hesitation, I commend them to you as good spiritual food for the soul. When it comes to reading Swinnock, the place to begin is with the three treatises that I have highlighted in this volume: *The Incomparableness of God*, *The Door of Salvation Opened by the Key of Regeneration*, and *The Christian Man's Calling*. There are certainly others worthy of your time. I will mention but three.

In *Heaven and Hell Epitomized*, Swinnock takes as his text the words of the apostle Paul: "For to me to live is Christ, and to die is gain."[3] Based upon these words, he endeavors to portray "life in Christ, or true Christianity, with the matchless, endless felicity that accompanieth it."[4] He speaks of the Christian's "privative gain by death," namely, freedom from the evil of sin and suffering. He also speaks of the Christian's "positive gain by death," namely, the company of perfect Christians, the nearest communion with Christ, and the immediate fruition of God. Swinnock declares, "As nothing that a godly man giveth God will content him, unless he give God himself, so nothing which God giveth a godly man will satisfy him, unless God giveth himself to him."[5]

In *The Sinner's Last Sentence*, Swinnock focuses upon Christ's warning: "Depart from me, ye cursed into everlasting fire, prepared for the devil and his angels: for I was an hungered, and ye gave me no

---

3. Philippians 1:21.

4. Swinnock, *Heaven and Hell Epitomized*, 3:214.

5. Swinnock, *Heaven and Hell Epitomized*, 3:249.

meat: I was thirsty, and ye gave me no drink."[6] Here, Swinnock sets forth four doctrines: (1) "That a great part of wicked men's punishment in the other world will consist in their departure from the presence of Christ," (2) "That the wicked shall in the other world depart from Christ into fire," (3) "That the punishment of the wicked in the other world will be everlasting," and (4) "That sins of omission are dangerous and damnable."[7] In this book, Swinnock provides a sobering treatment of a subject that is downplayed (and oftentimes openly denied) in our day: the eternal conscious punishment of unbelievers in hell.

In *The Fading of the Flesh*, Swinnock expounds the words of the psalmist: "My flesh and my heart faileth: But God is the strength of my heart, and my portion for ever."[8] He proceeds to explain how God comforts the Christian in death, stating, "This all-sufficient, suitable, and eternal God is the saint's peculiar portion, and therefore causeth infinite satisfaction."[9] In a word, God is "the sweetest love, the richest mercy, the surest friend, the chiefest good, the greatest beauty, the highest honour, and the fullest happiness."[10] Therefore, He alone is the Christian's comfort—not only in death but in all circumstances of life. This practical and pastoral treatise is full of comforting and challenging insights.

---

6. Matthew 25:41–42.

7. Swinnock*, The Sinner's Last Sentence*, 5:278, 297, 303, 317.

8. Psalm 73:26.

9. Swinnock, *Fading of the Flesh*, 4:11.

10. Swinnock, *Fading of the Flesh*, 4:28.

As you read Swinnock, you will discover that he employs the same approach in all his works: he interprets his text; he then explains several doctrines arising from his text; he then applies those doctrines by way of "uses" (information, examination, exhortation, and consolation).[11] In Swinnock's own words, this "plain" approach is best designed for "convincing the judgment, and working upon the affections."[12] When you read his works prayerfully and thoughtfully, you will find it to be so.

Bibliography of Swinnock's writings:

The Life and Death of Mr. Thomas Wilson, Minister of Maidstone, in the County of Kent, M.A. London, 1672.

The Works of George Swinnock. 5 vols. Edited by J. Nichol. London, 1868; rpt., Edinburgh: Banner of Truth, 1992. These *Works* include:

- *Christian Man's Calling; or, A treatise of making religion ones business: Parts 1, 2, 3* (1661–1665).

- *Door of Salvation Opened by the Key of Regeneration; or, A treatise containing the nature, necessity, marks*

---

11. By and large, the Puritans (including Swinnock) adopt William Perkins' four-step approach to preaching: (1) read the text, (2) expound the text, (3) derive several points of doctrine from the text, and (4) apply the points of doctrine to all of life. See William Perkins, *Arte of Prophesying; or, A treatise concerning the sacred and onely true manner and methode of preaching* in *The Works of William Perkins: Vol. 2* (London: John Legate, 1608). It is no surprise to find the same approach in their writings, which are for the most part published sermons.

12. Swinnock, *Christian Man's Calling,* 1:147.

and means of regeneration: as also the duty of the regenerate (1660).

- *Fading of the Flesh and Flourishing of the Faith; or, One cast for eternity: with the only way to throw it well: as also the gracious persons incomparable portion* (1662).

- *Gods Are Men; or, Magistrates are mortal* (1657).

- *Men Are Gods; or, The dignity of magistracy, and the duty of the magistrate* (1659).

- Ουρανοϖ και ταρταροϖ; *or, Heaven and hell epitomized: the true Christian characterized, as also an exhortation with motives, means and directions to be speedy and serious about the work of conversion* (1658).

- *Pastor's Farewell and wish of welfare to his people; or, A valedictory sermon* (1660).

- *Sinner's last sentence to eternal punishment, for sins of omission: wherein is discovered the nature, causes and cure of those sins* (1675).

- *Treatise of the incomparableness of God in his being, attributes, works and word: opened and applied* (1672).

Lord, why should I contented be,
whilst I am thus absent from thee?
Can there be day without the sun,
or bodies live when souls are gone?

Thou art my Sun, my Soul, and I
absent from that do daily die.
What do I here, when all's above,
that is deserving of my love?

My God, my Christ, my friends are there,
my heart, my hopes, what do I here?
O let my heaven-born soul expire
itself in sallies, and desire.

Only to rest, and make its stay,
where thou art all in all for ay.
O come thou down with speed to me,
or take me quickly up to thee.

(From a poem "on the much lamented death of my sincerely honoured and beloved friend Mr. Thomas Wilson" in Swinnock, *Life and Death of Mr. Wilson*, 96)